the starving artist...

the eyes that feel, the hands that see

2014

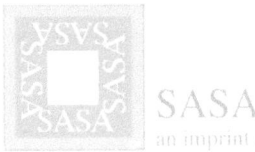

SASA™
an imprint of Little Acorn Associates, Inc.

the starving artist... 2014
the eyes that feel, the hands that see

©2014 SASA™

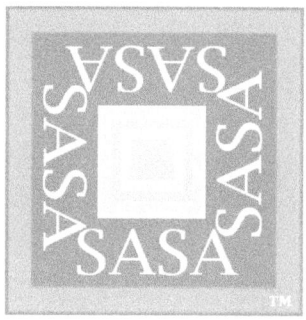

SASA™ is an imprint of little acorn associates, inc.

published by
little acorn associates, inc.
all rights reserved.

publication number: SASA-0614
ISBN 978-1-937257-71-2

all image copyrights remain with each individual artist

no portion or portions of this publication may be copied or reproduced in any format
whatsoever without verified written permission from the publisher.

the starving artist... 2014
the eyes that feel, the hands that see

dedicated to all who create

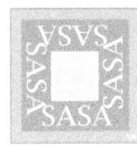

contents

the eyes that feel, the hands that see—........ 1
hoyle, jesse................................. 2
juras, katherine............................. 6
teague, sarah................................ 9
stultz, bethany............................. 10
acosta, alicia.............................. 14
thomas, christpoher......................... 16
taber, rachel............................... 20
tisdell, suzanne............................ 22
teague, sarah............................... 25
belluardo, stephanie........................ 26
alphabetical listing of
   the eyes that feel,the hands that see....... 32

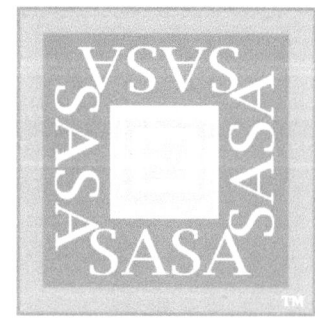

the eyes that feel, the hands that see

the eyes that feel, the hands that see
cannot be
empty vessels,
vacuums,
dormant,
exiled,
deprived,
abused,
inert,
barren,
hollow,
isolated,
discharged,
vacant,
unused,
suppressed,
desolate,
depleted,
void,
malnourished,
hungry,
starving—

lest prolonged starvation cause permanent damage,
and death of the visually charged—
    the painter, the sculptor, the designer,
    the photographer, the engraver, the illustrator,
    the artist, the maker,
    the eyes that feel, the hands that see—
ensues

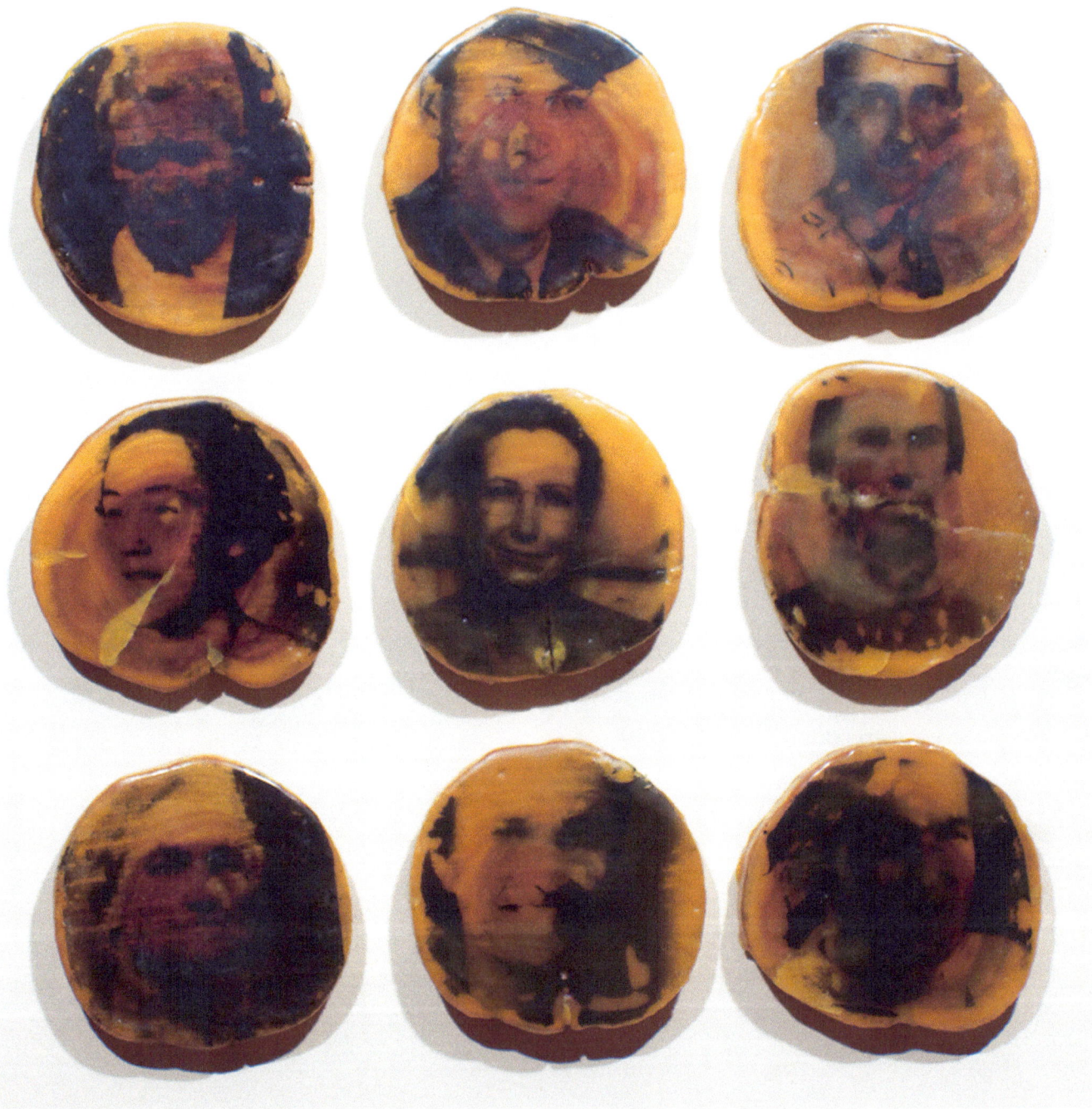

jesse hoyle

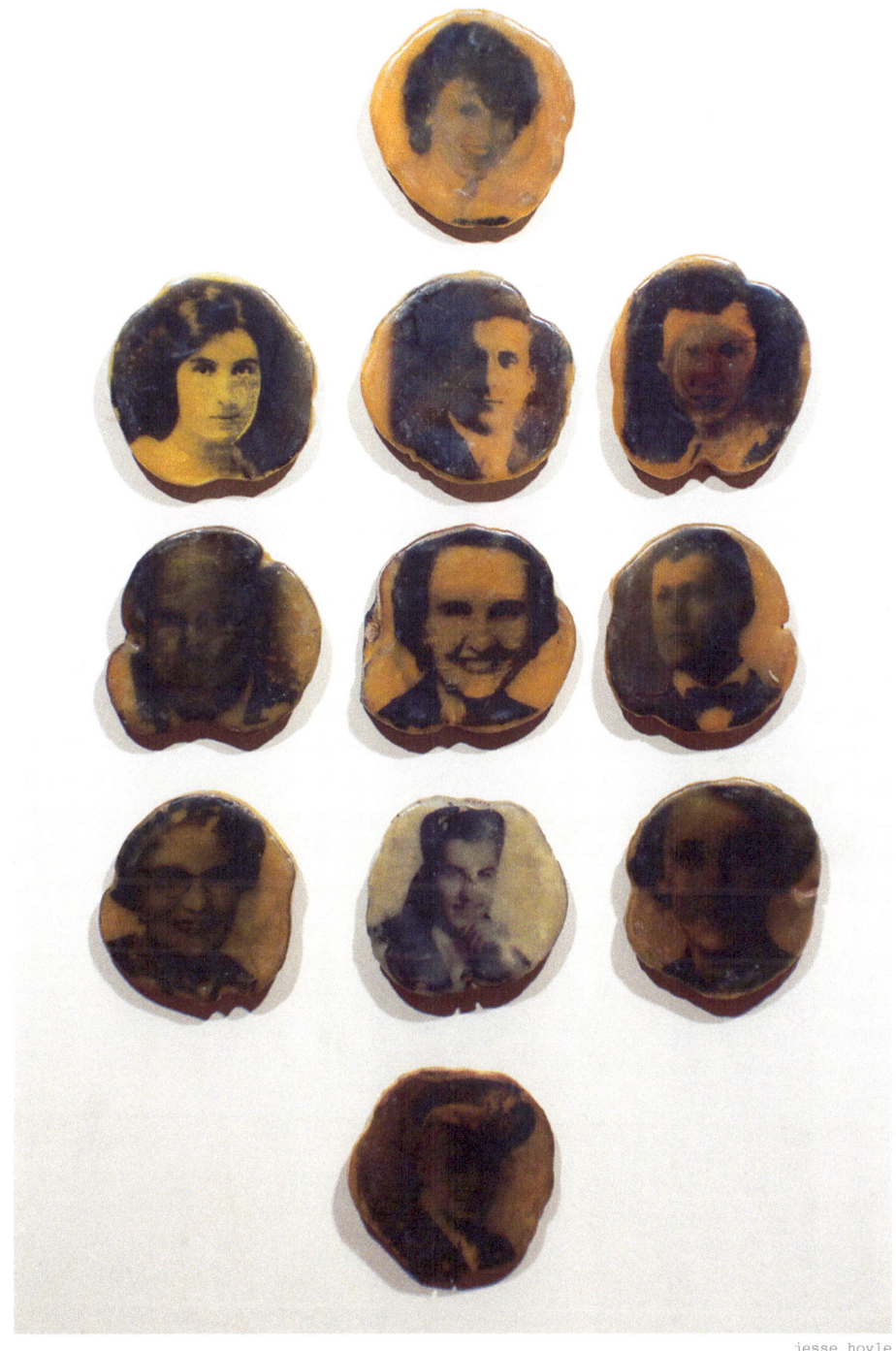

jesse hoyle

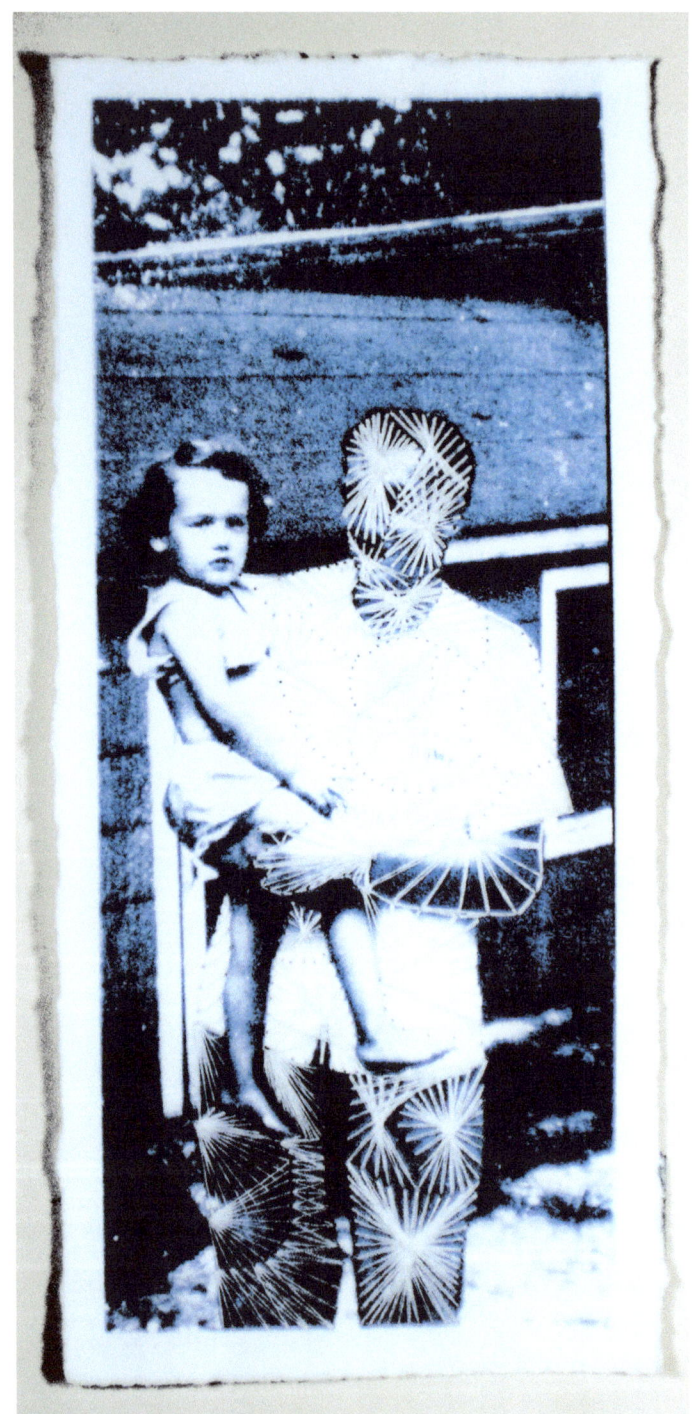

jesse hoyle

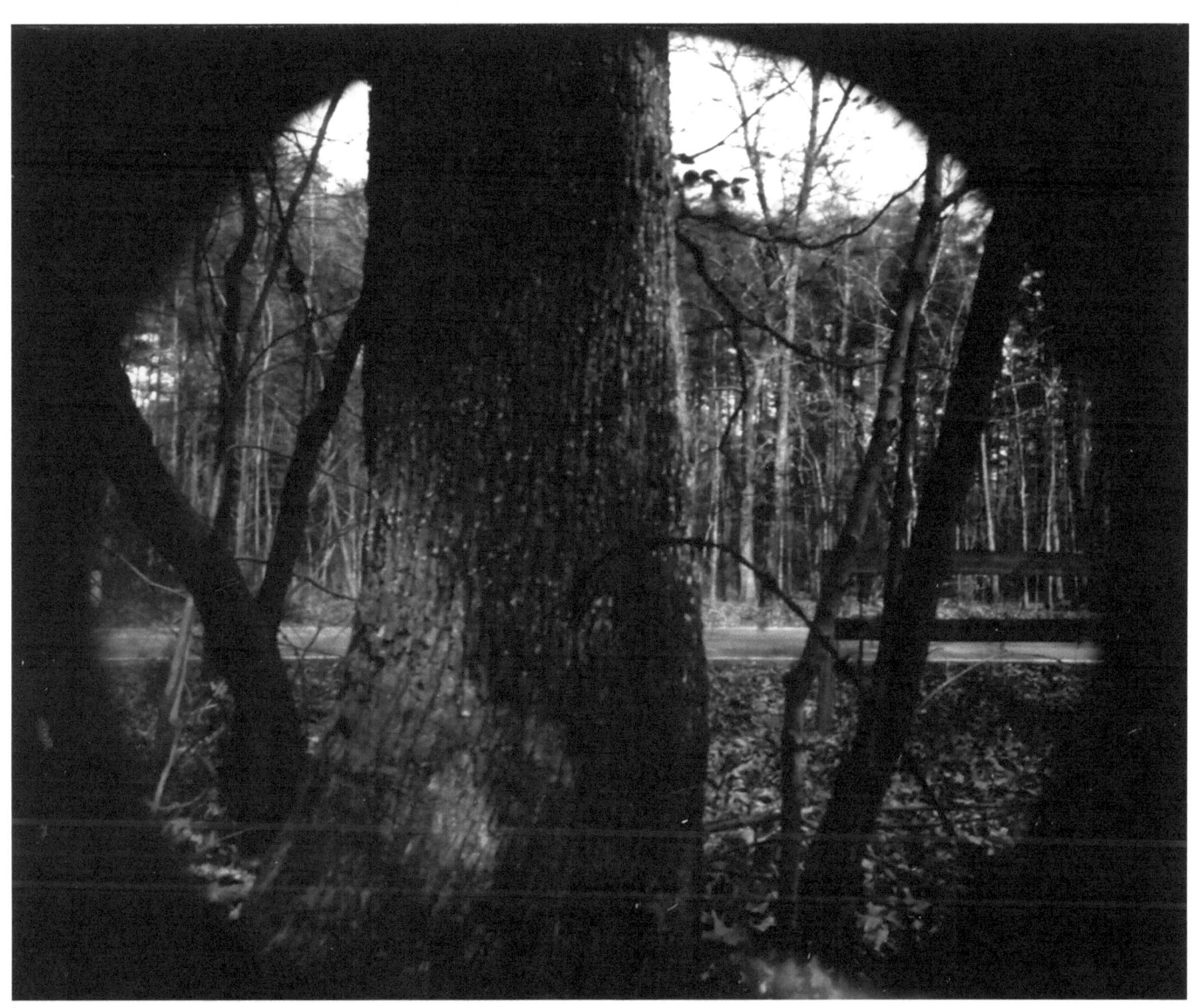

jesse hoyle

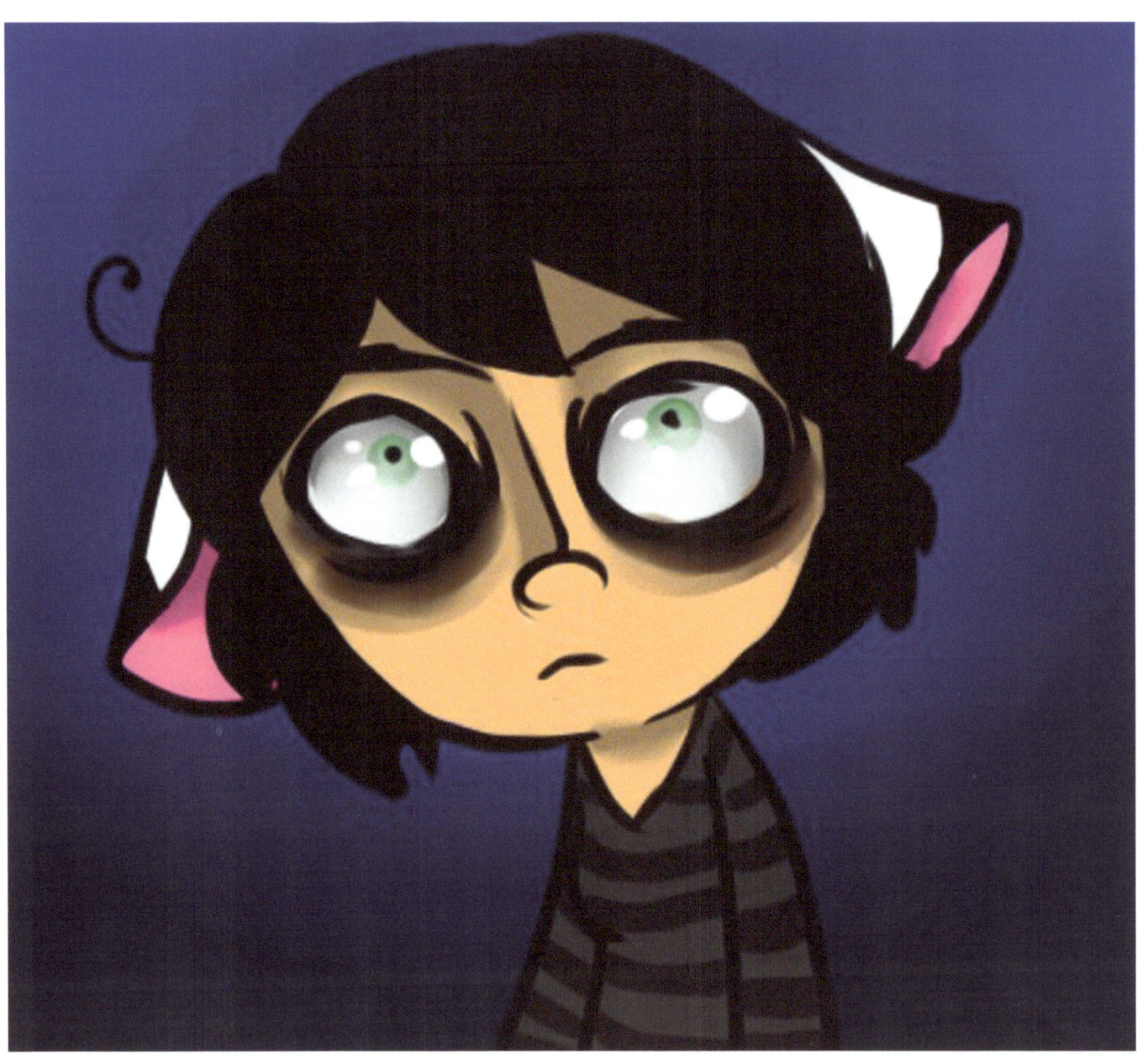

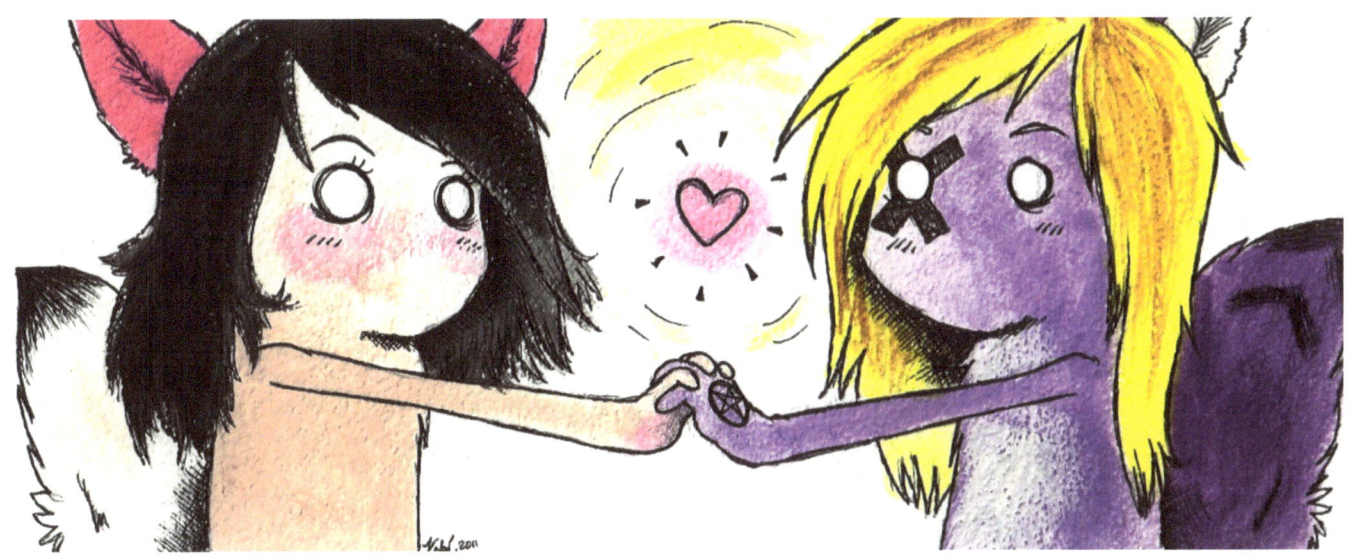

katherine juras

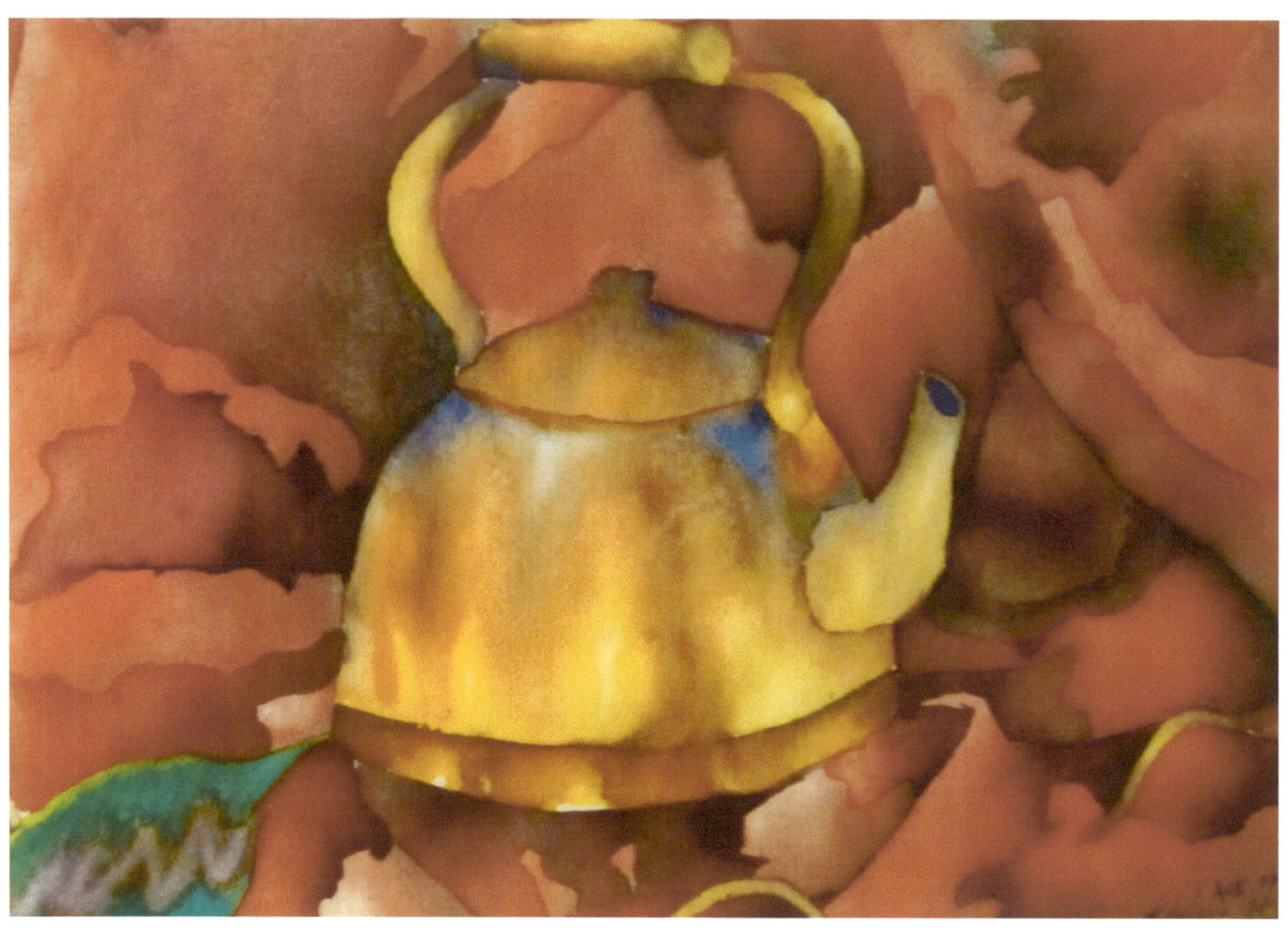

katherine juras

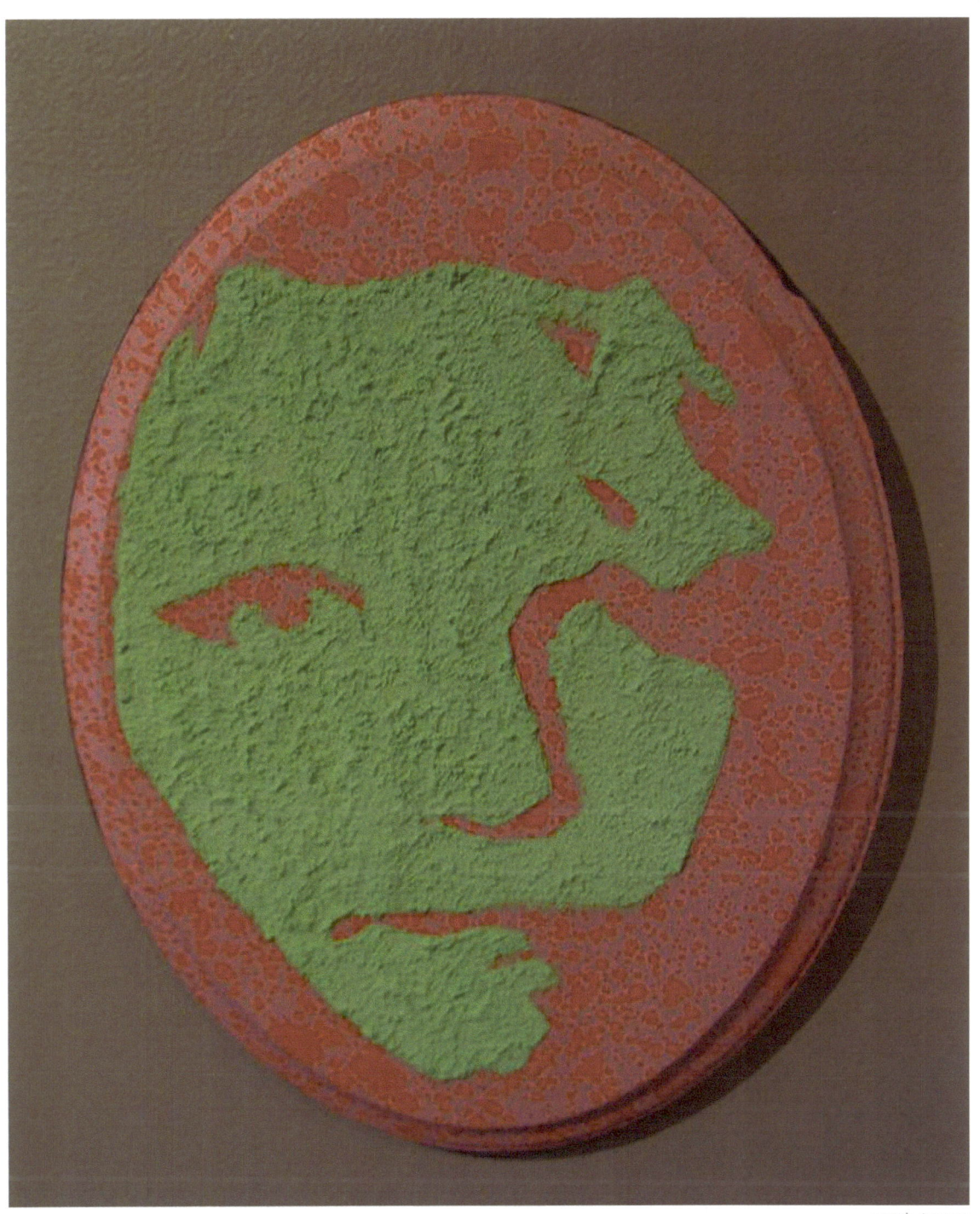

sarah teague

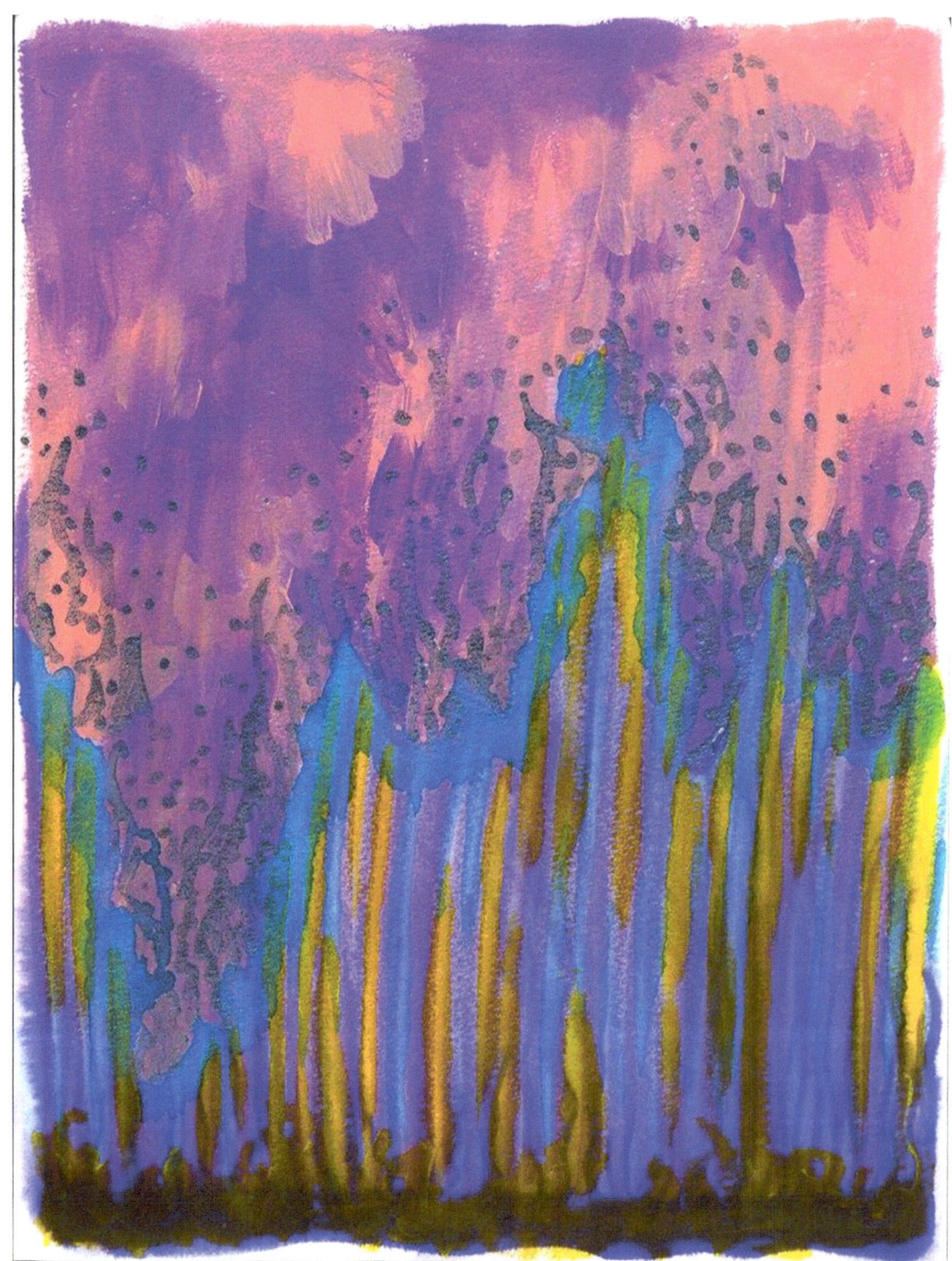

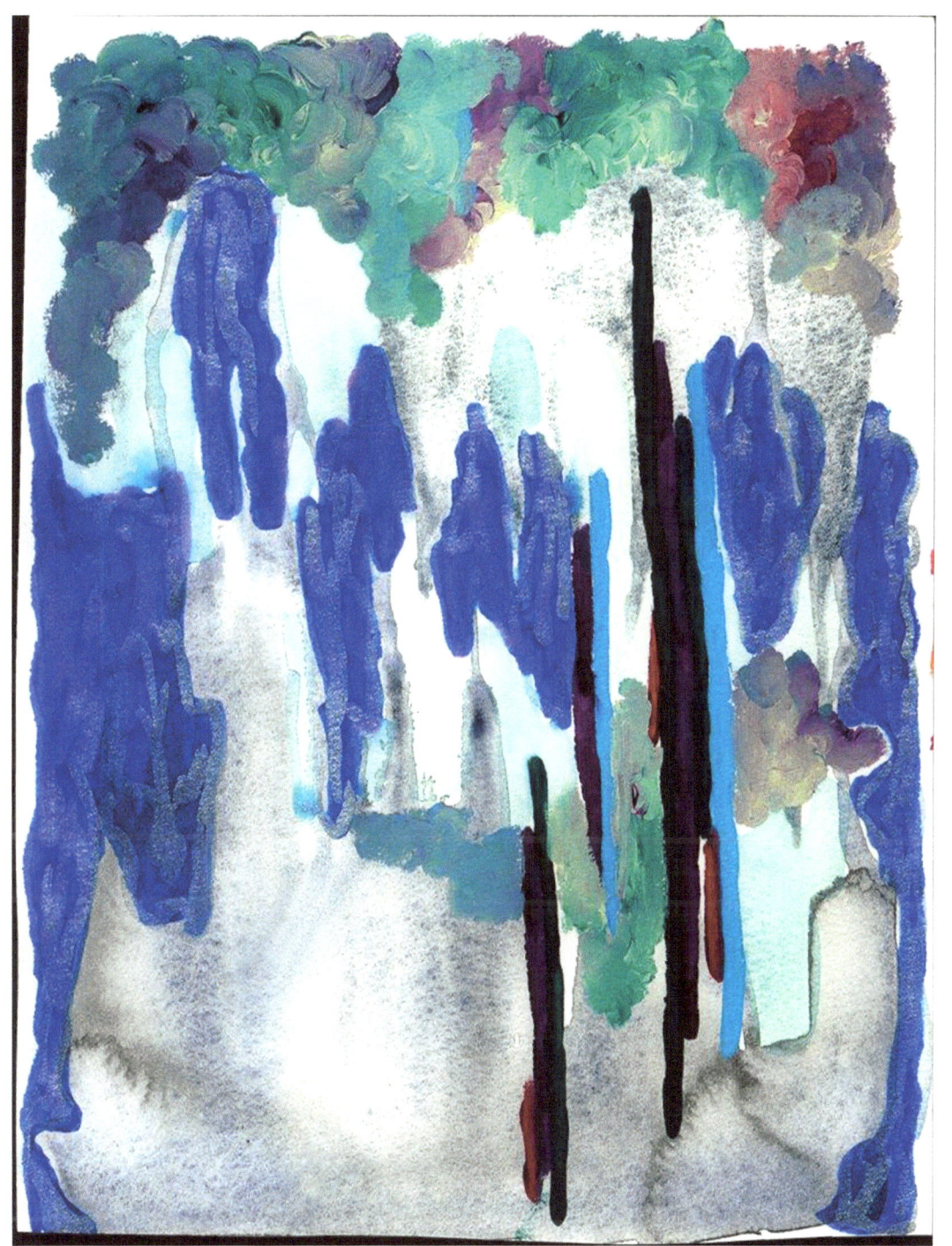

bethany stultz

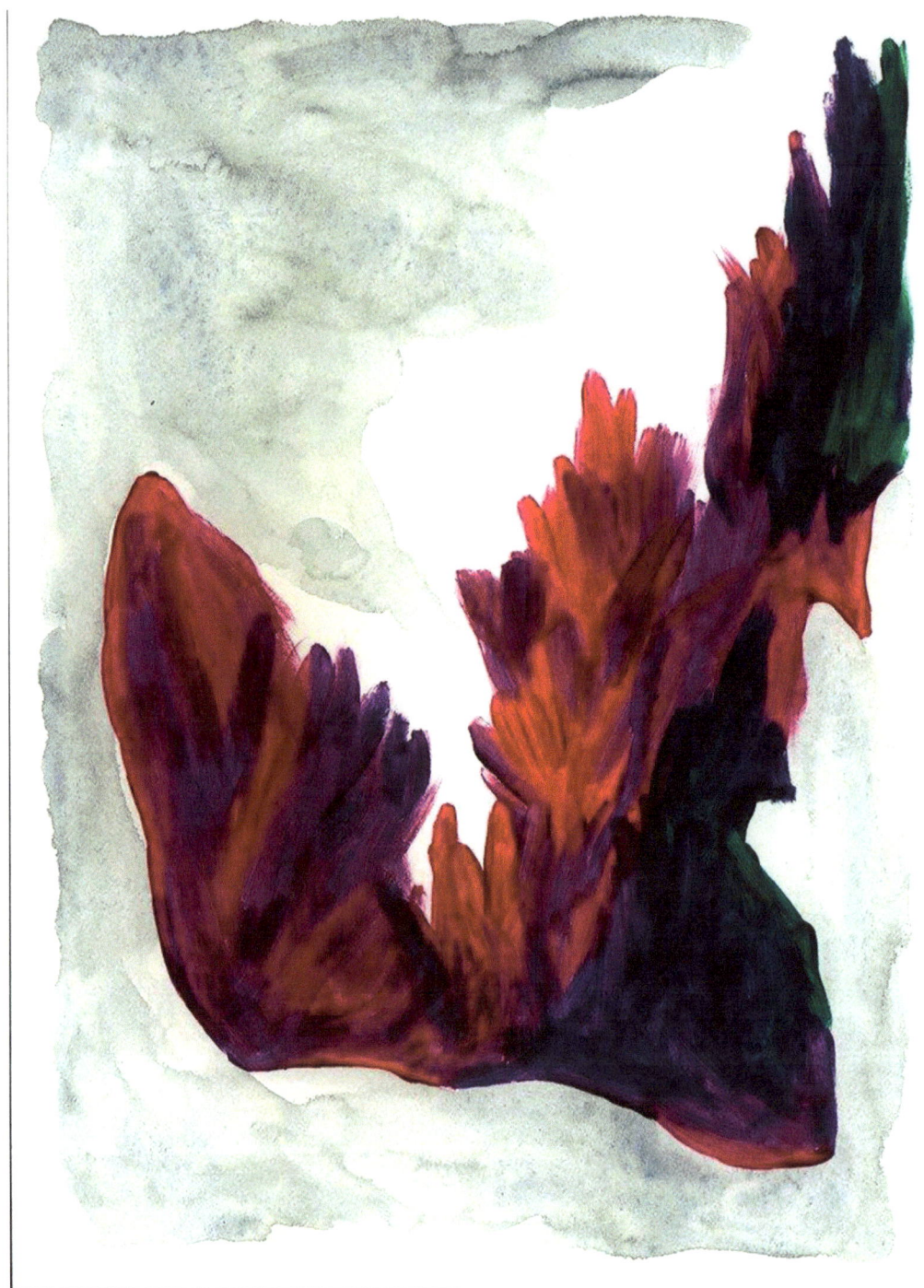

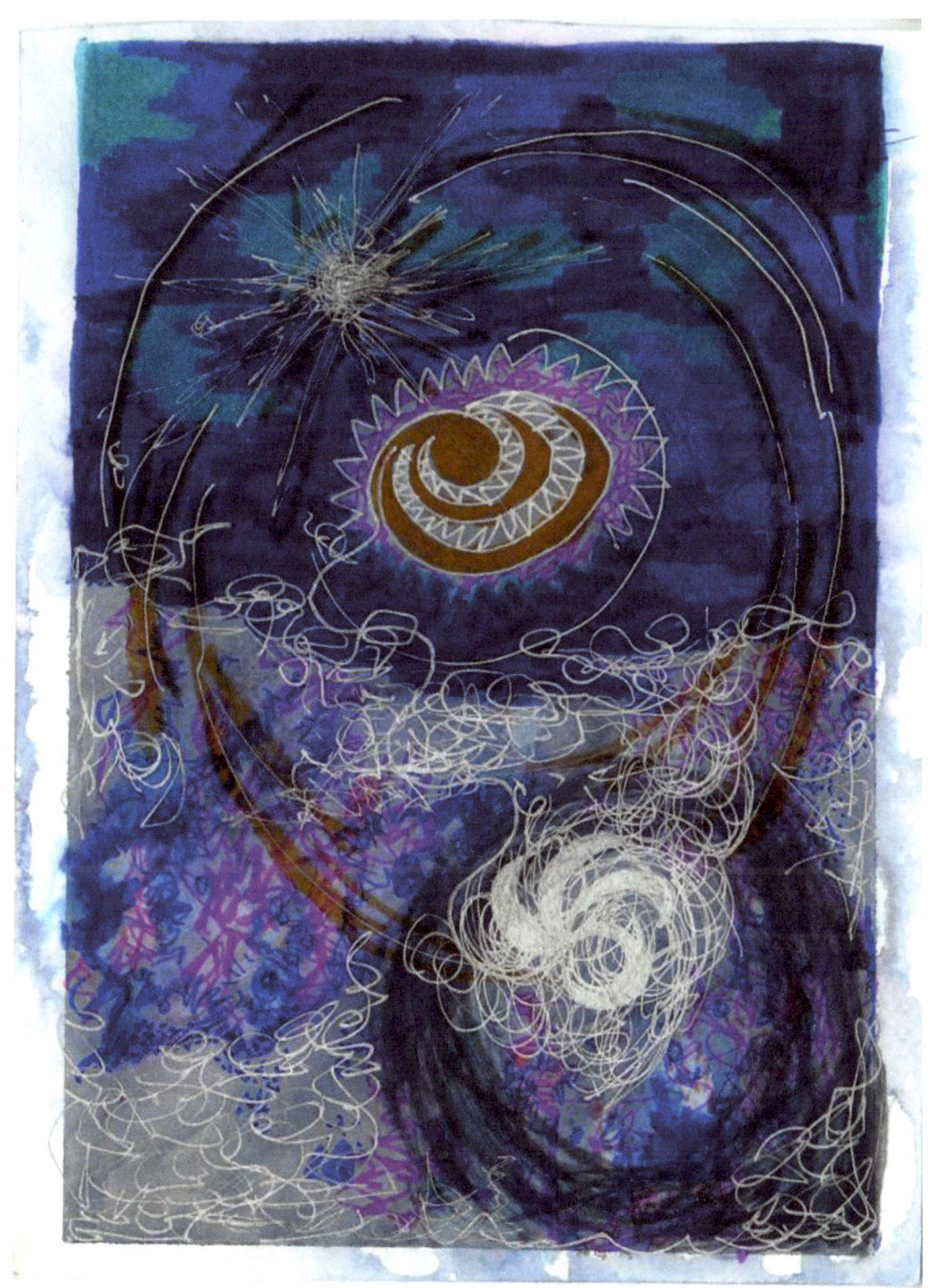

bethany stultz

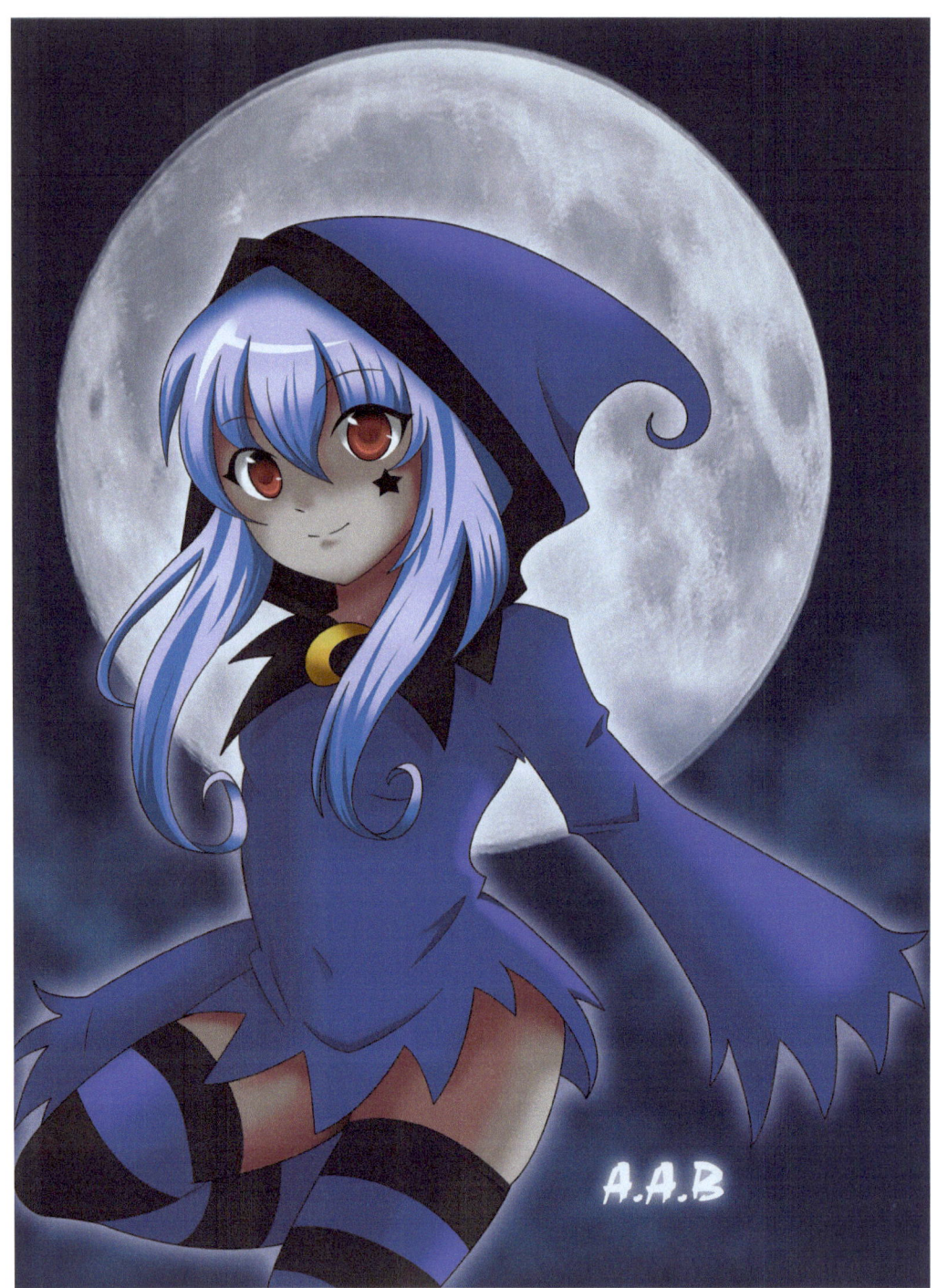

alicia acosta

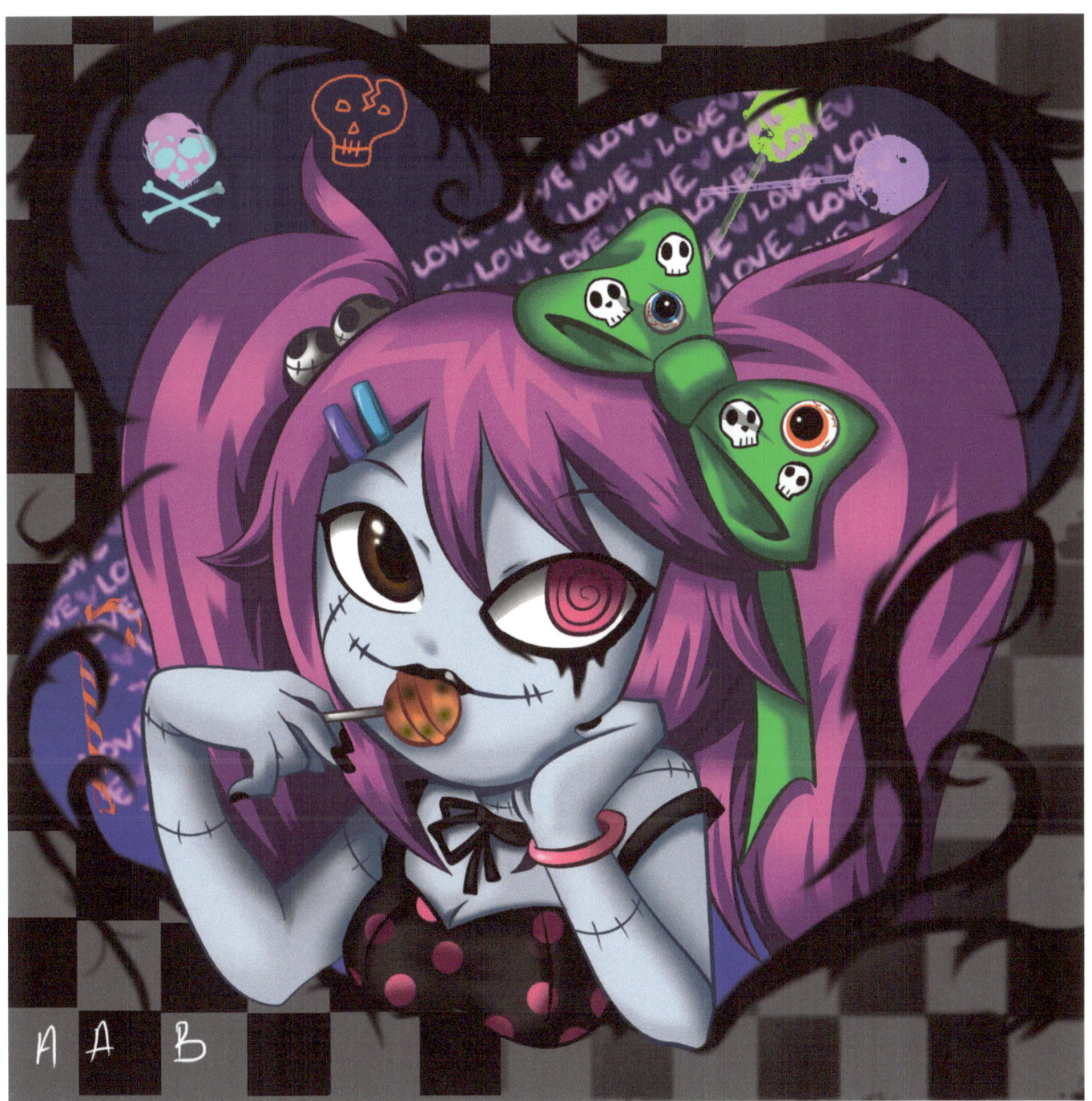

alicia acosta

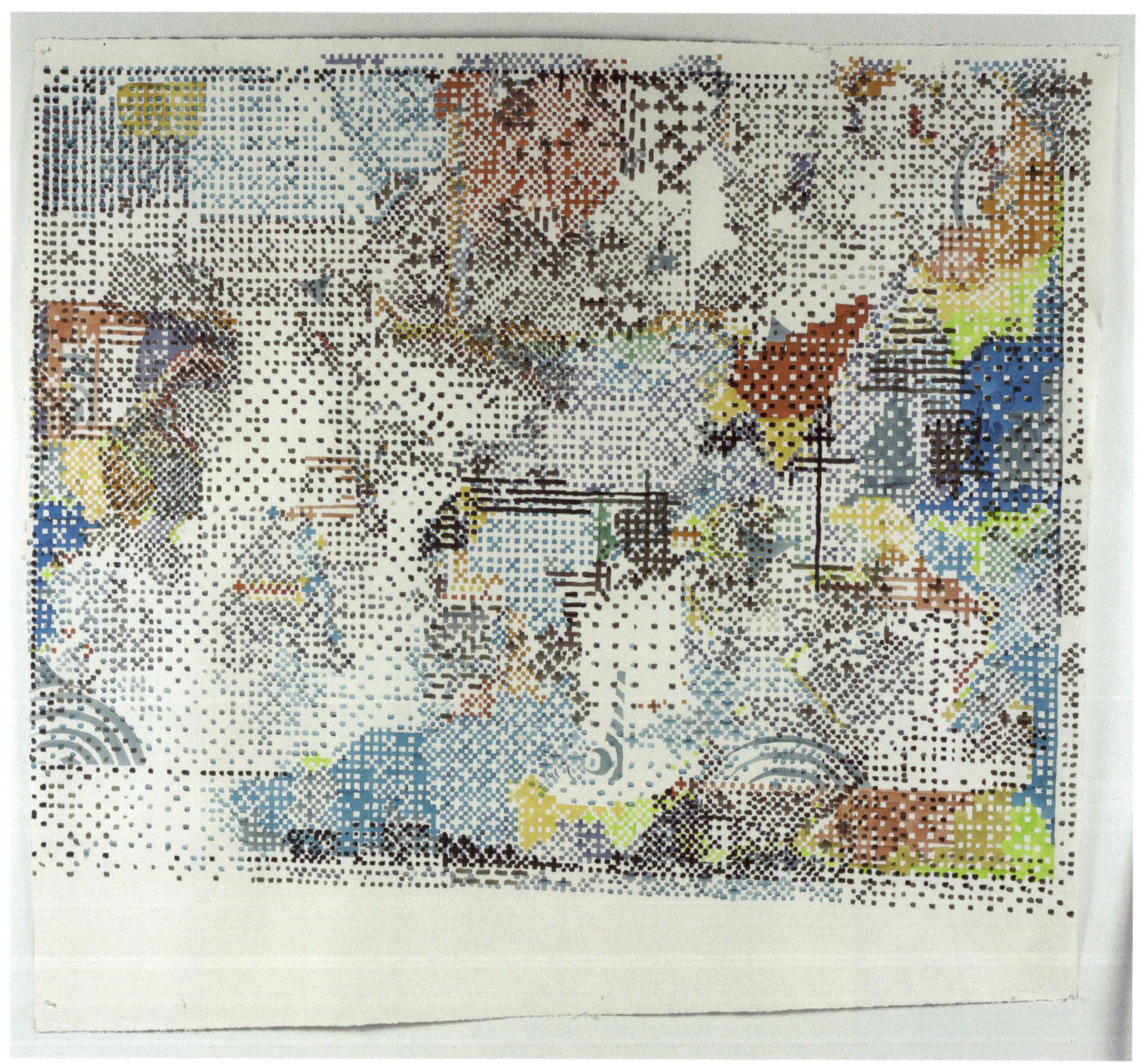

christopher thomas

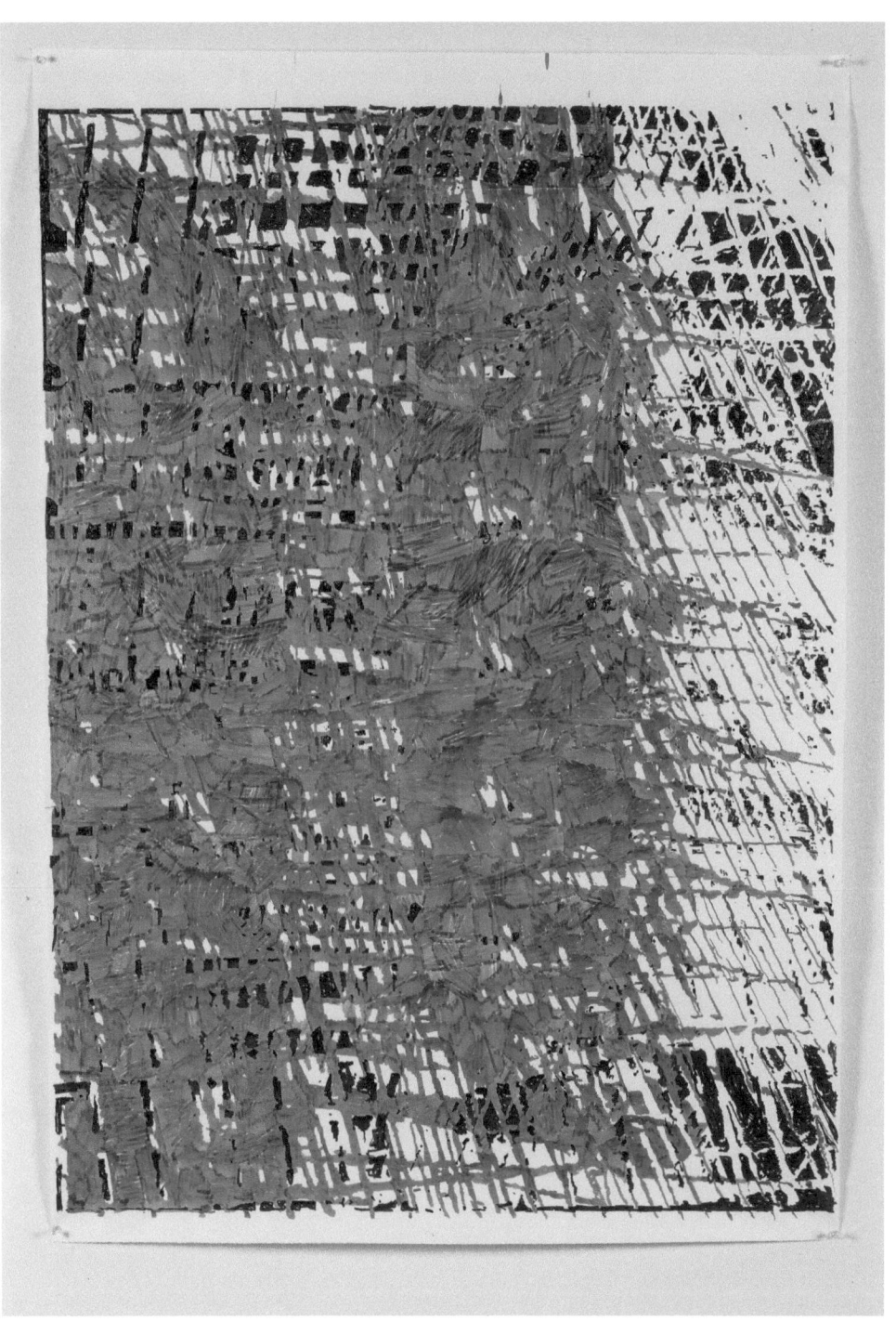

christopher thomas

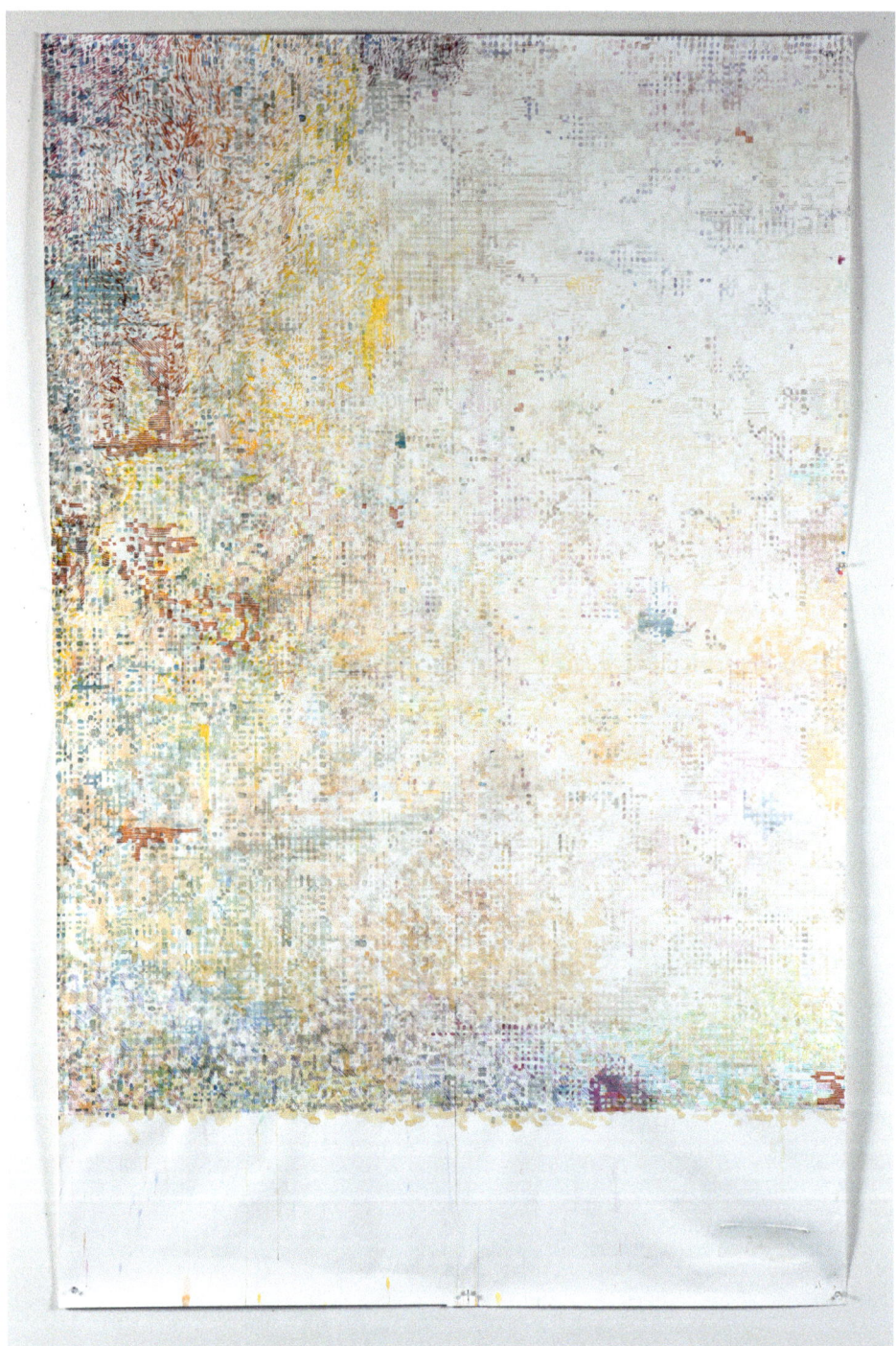

christopher thomas

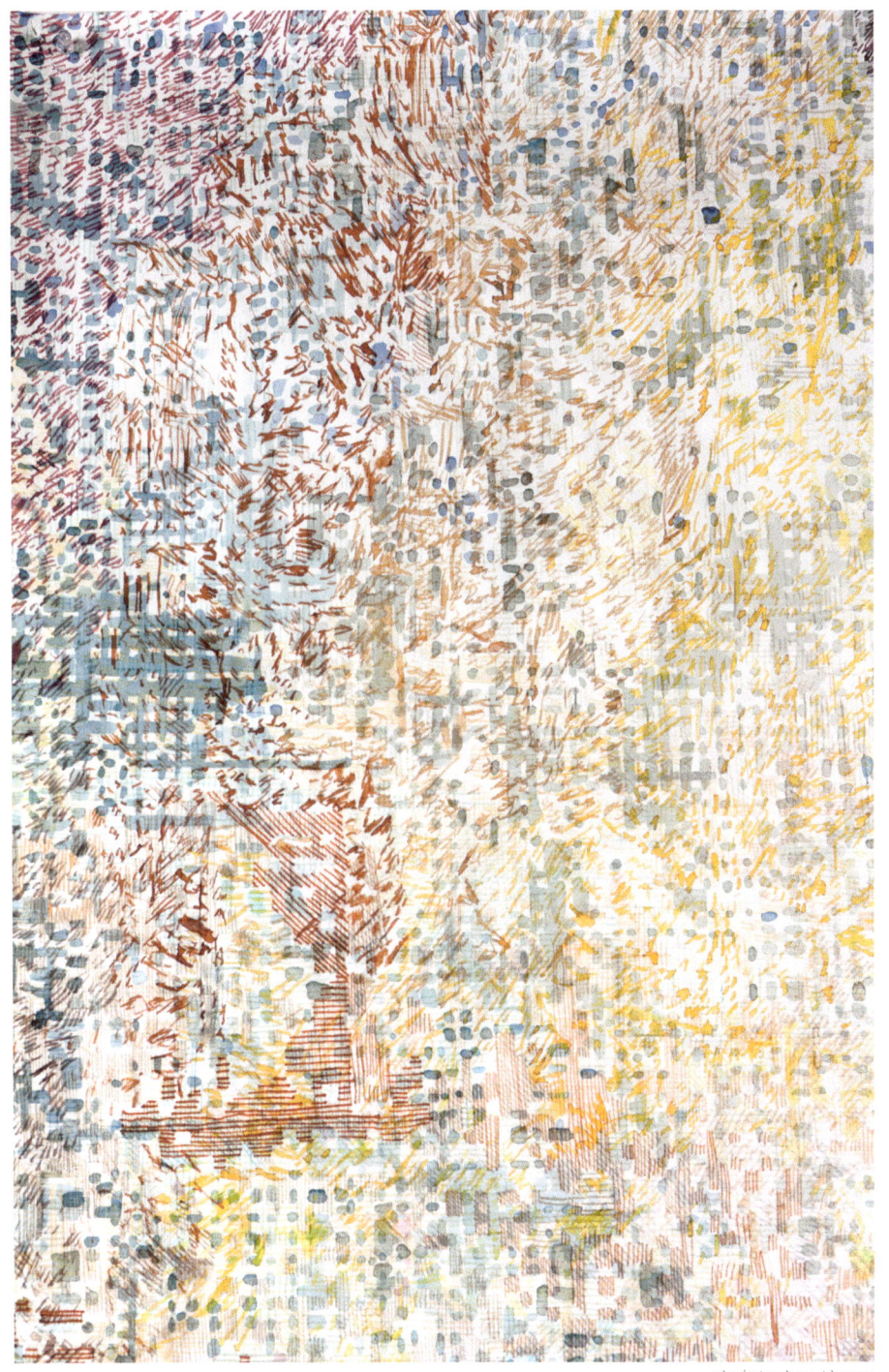

christopher thomas

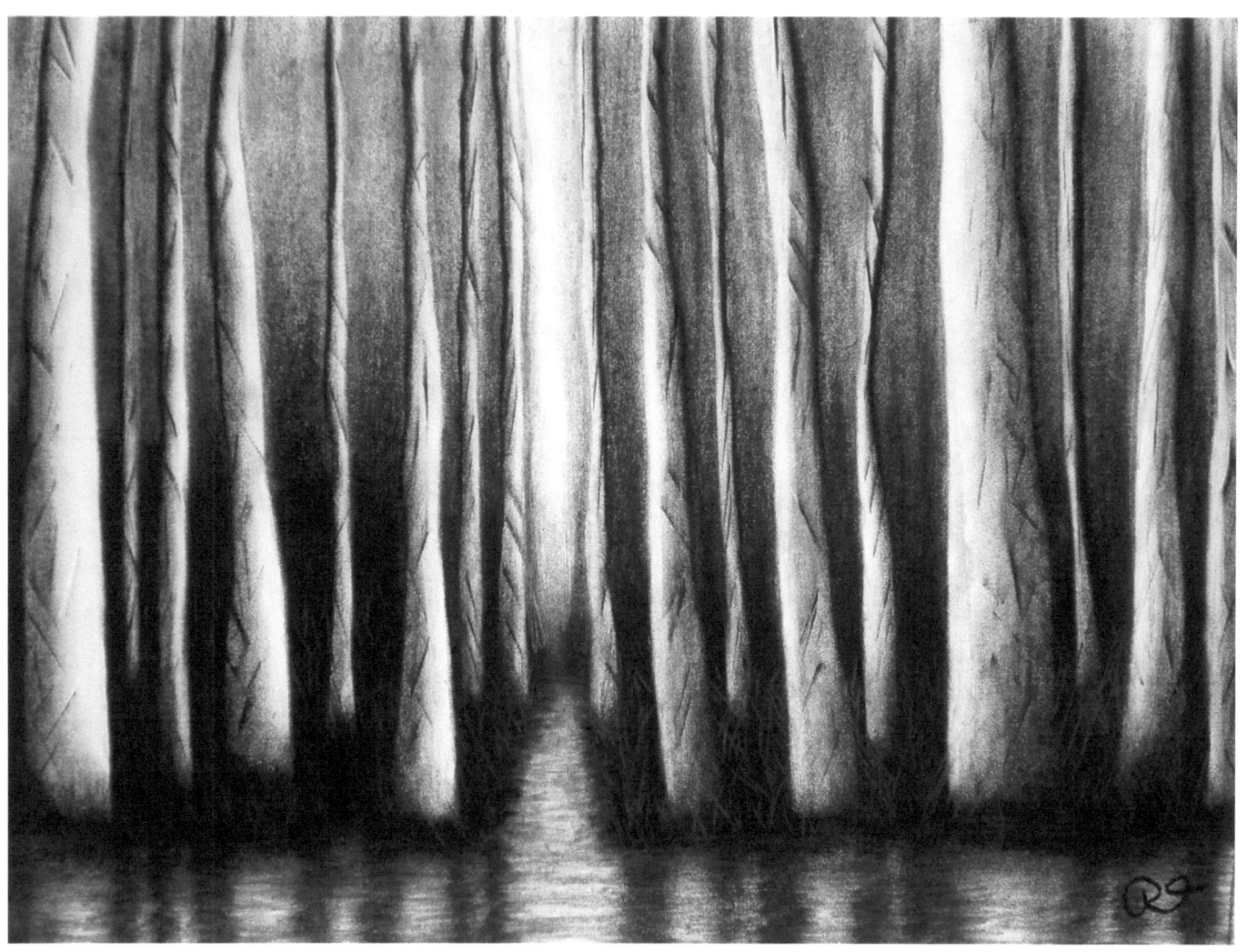

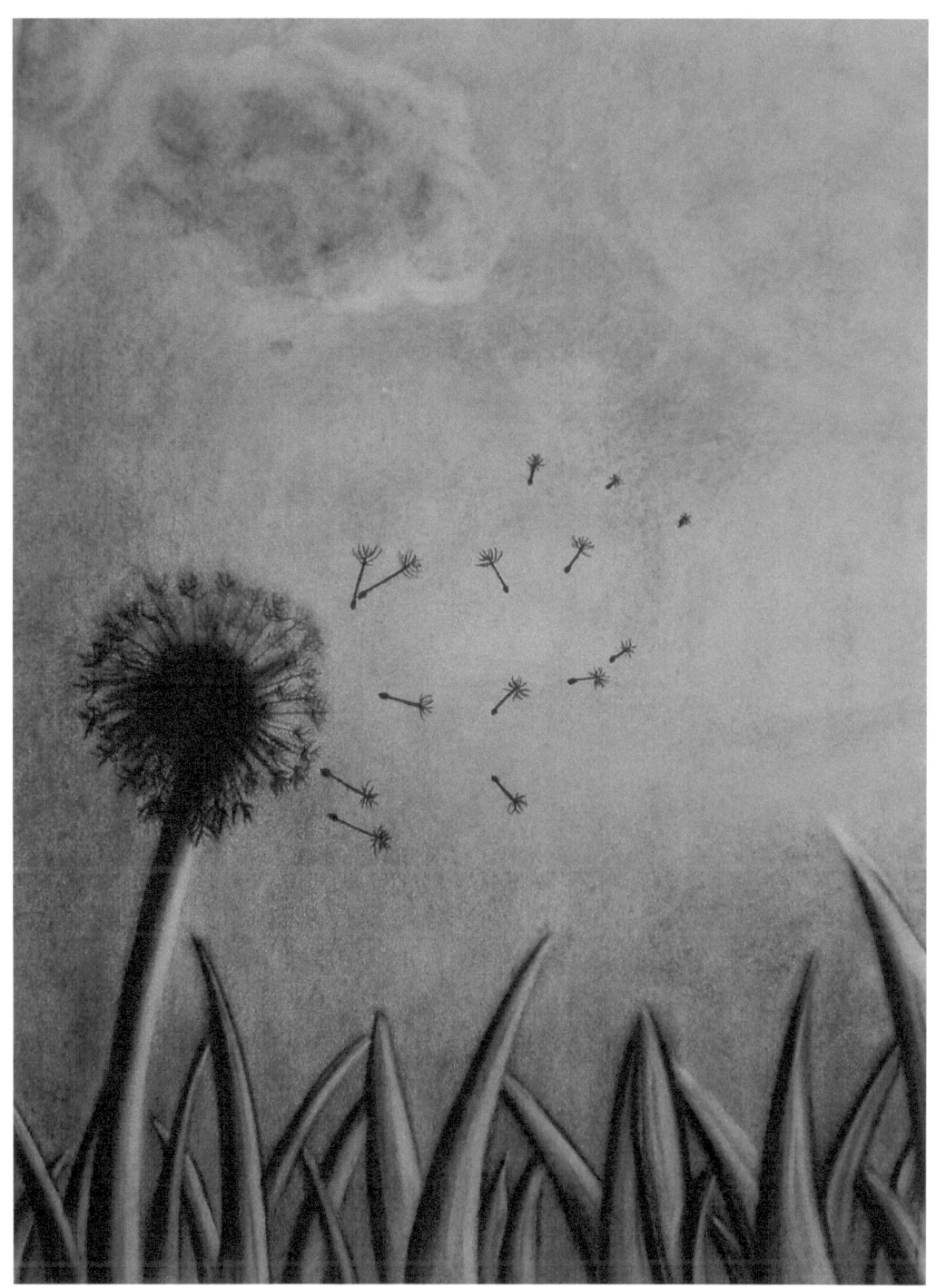

rachel taber

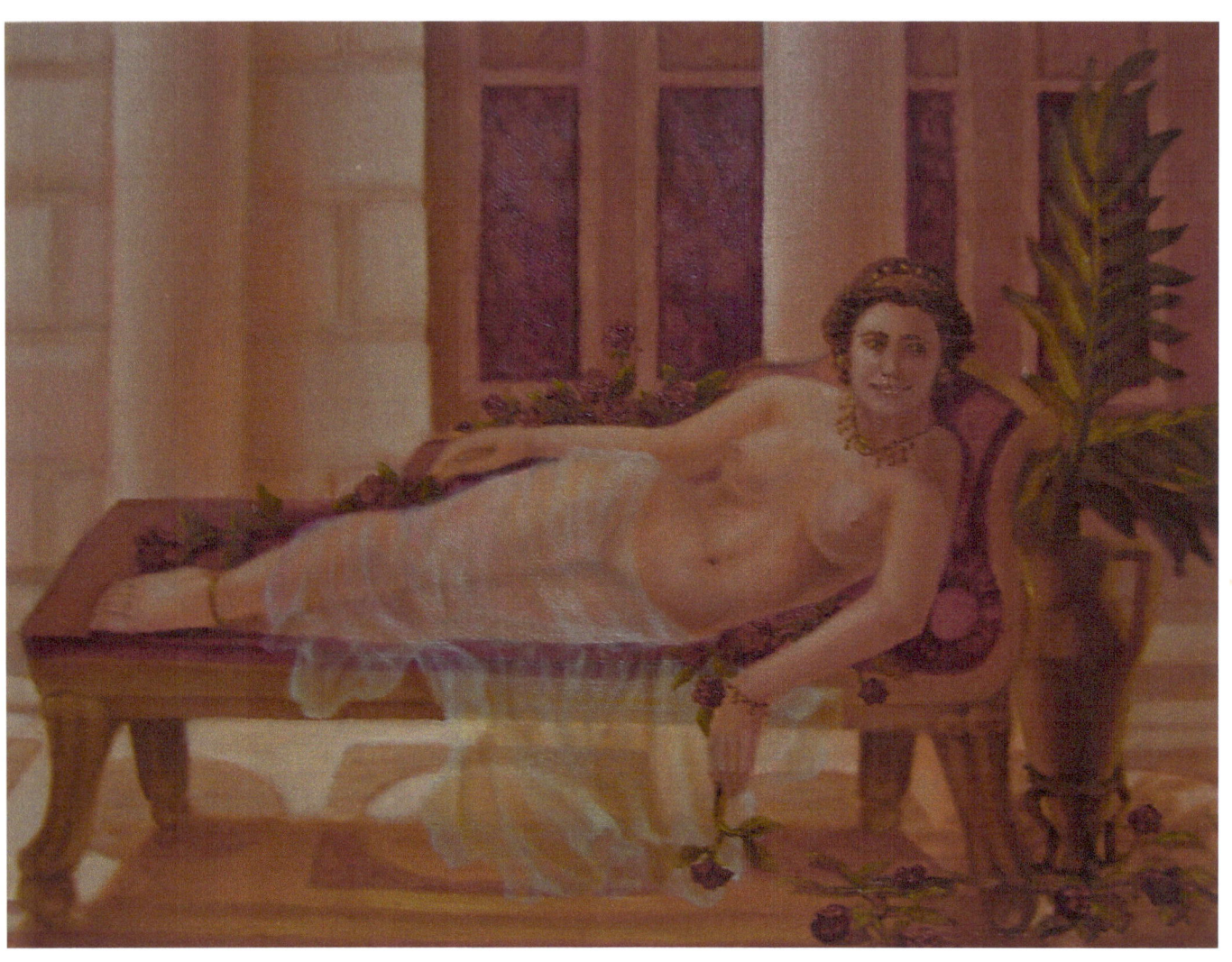

suzanne tisdell

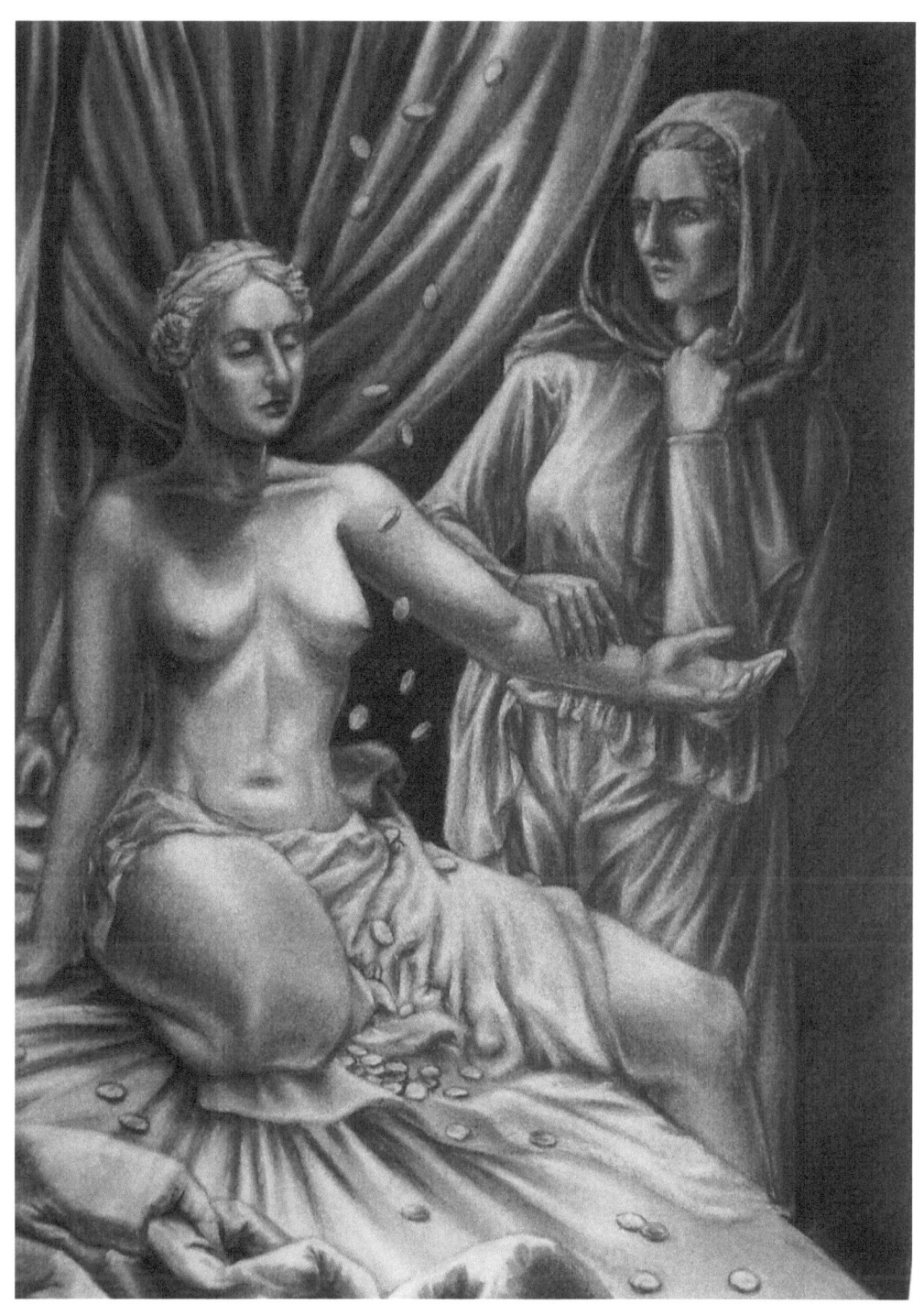

suzanne tisdell

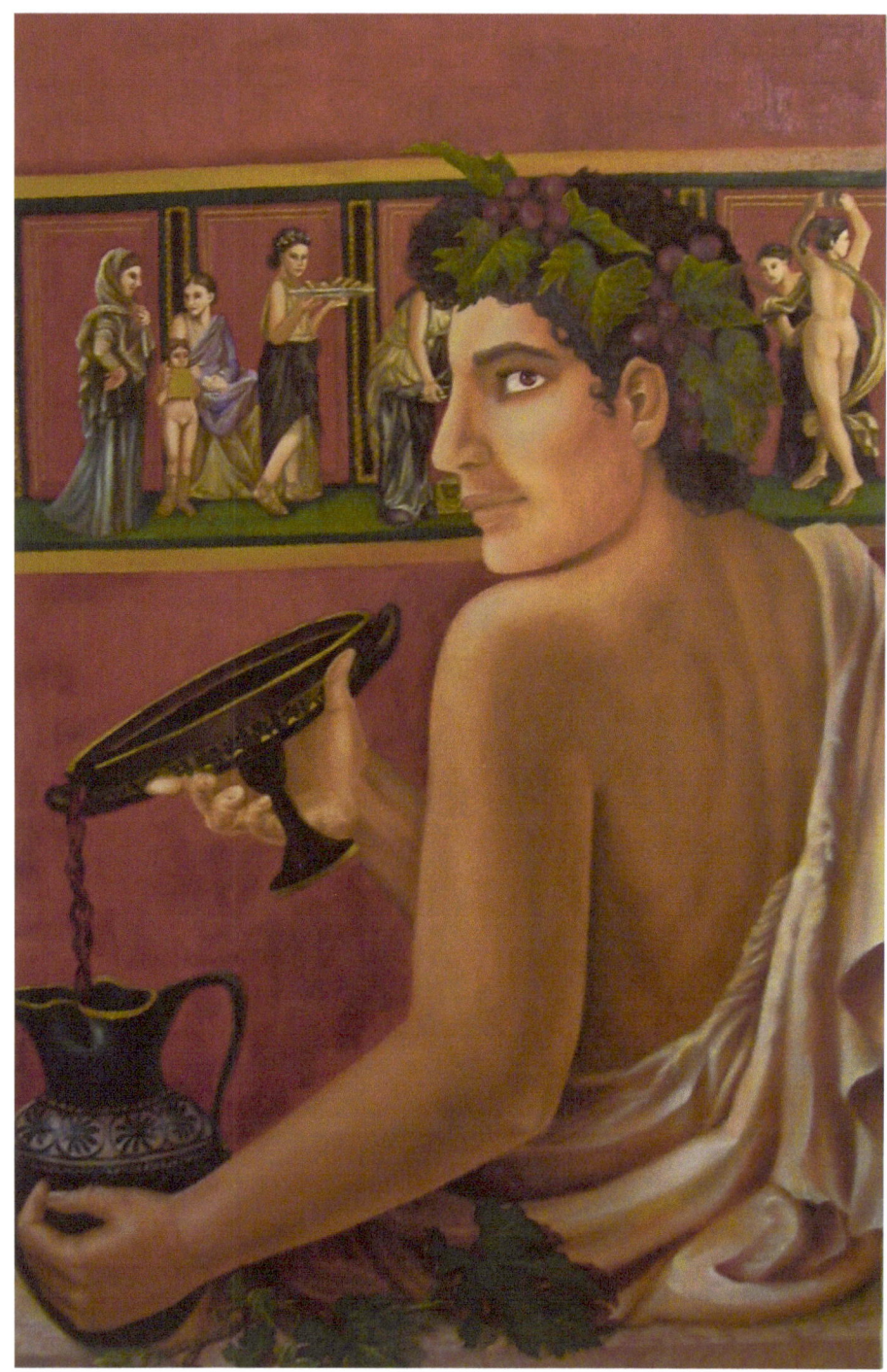

suzanne tisdell

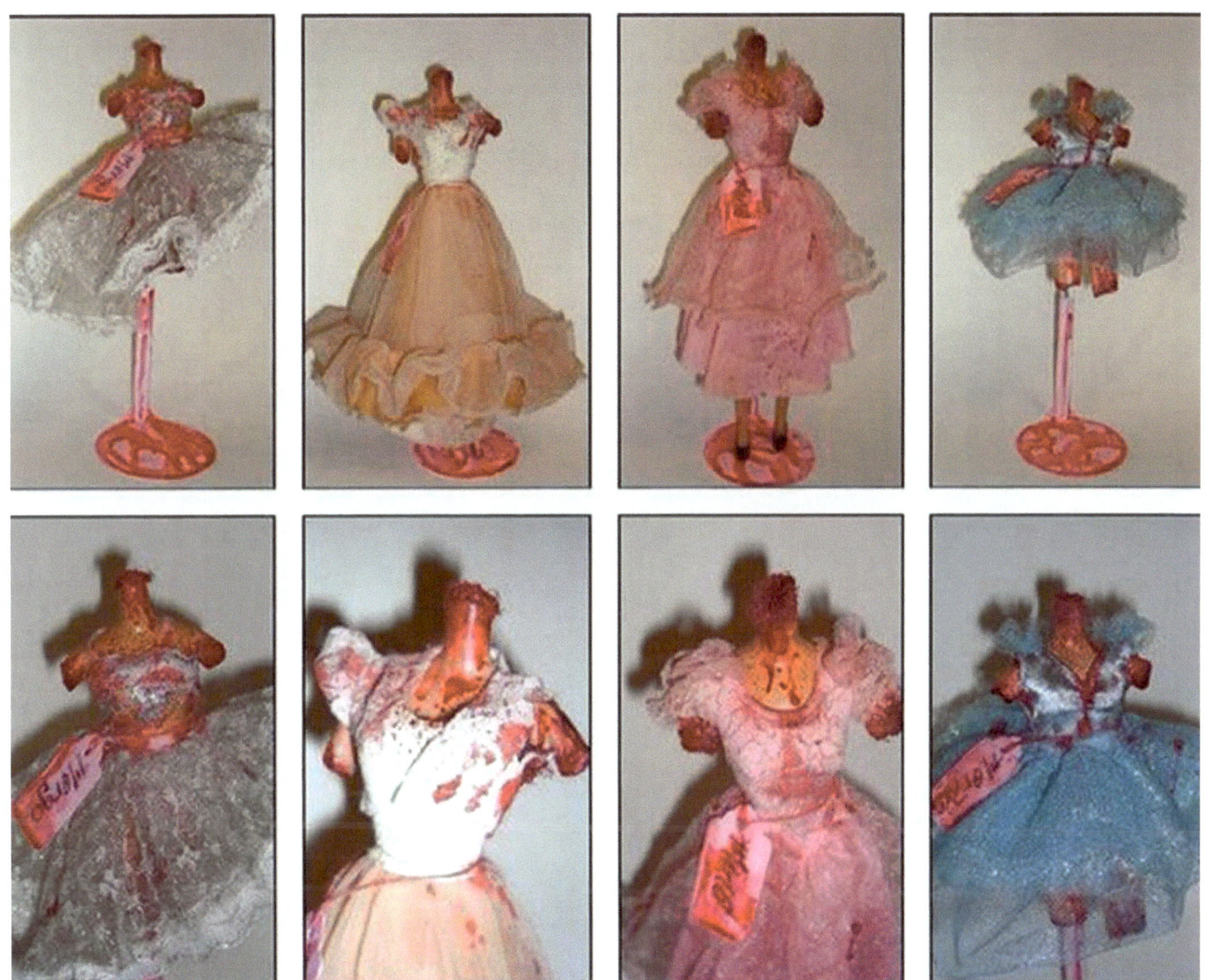

sarah teague

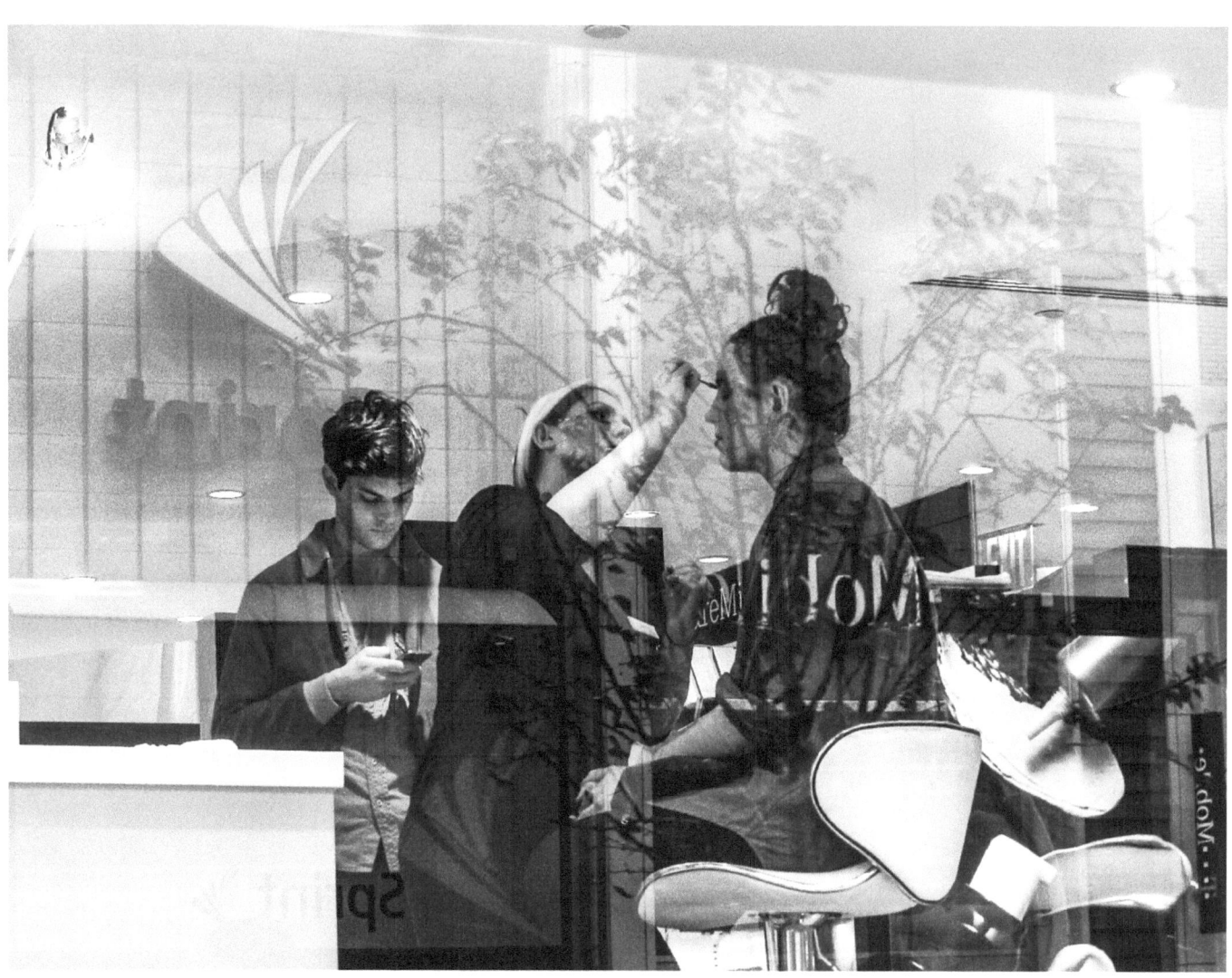

stephanie belluardo

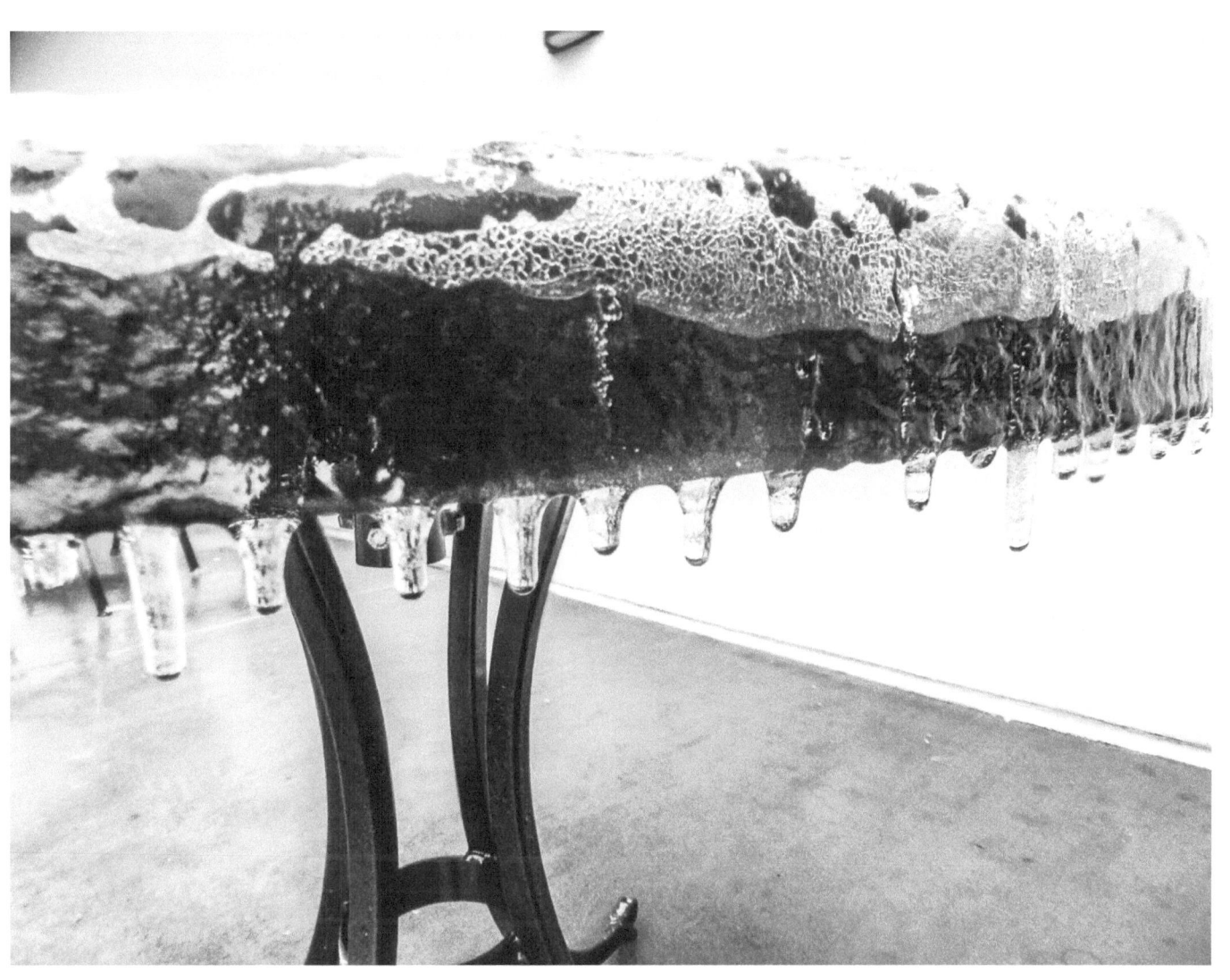

stephanie belluardo

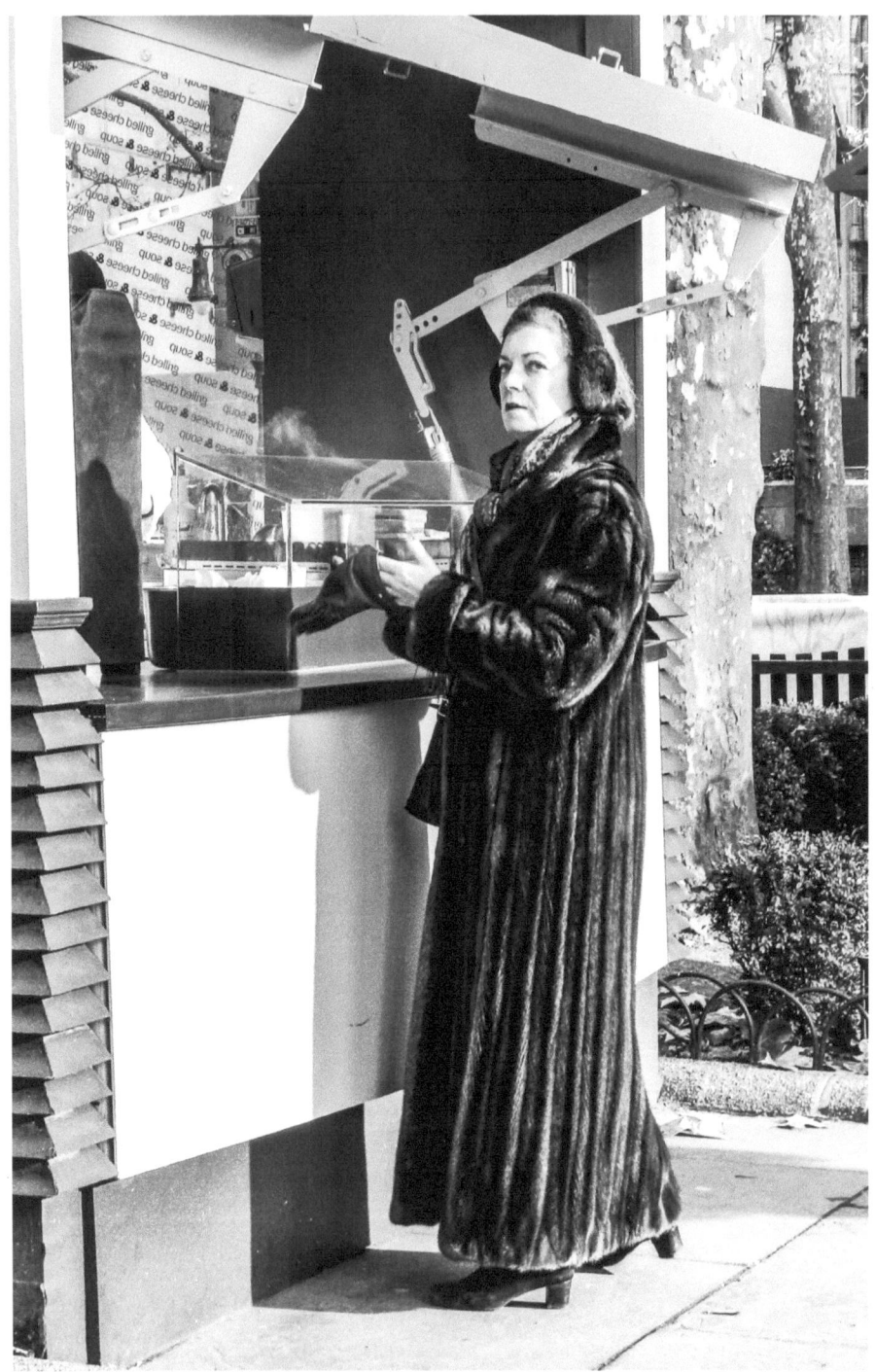

stephanie belluardo

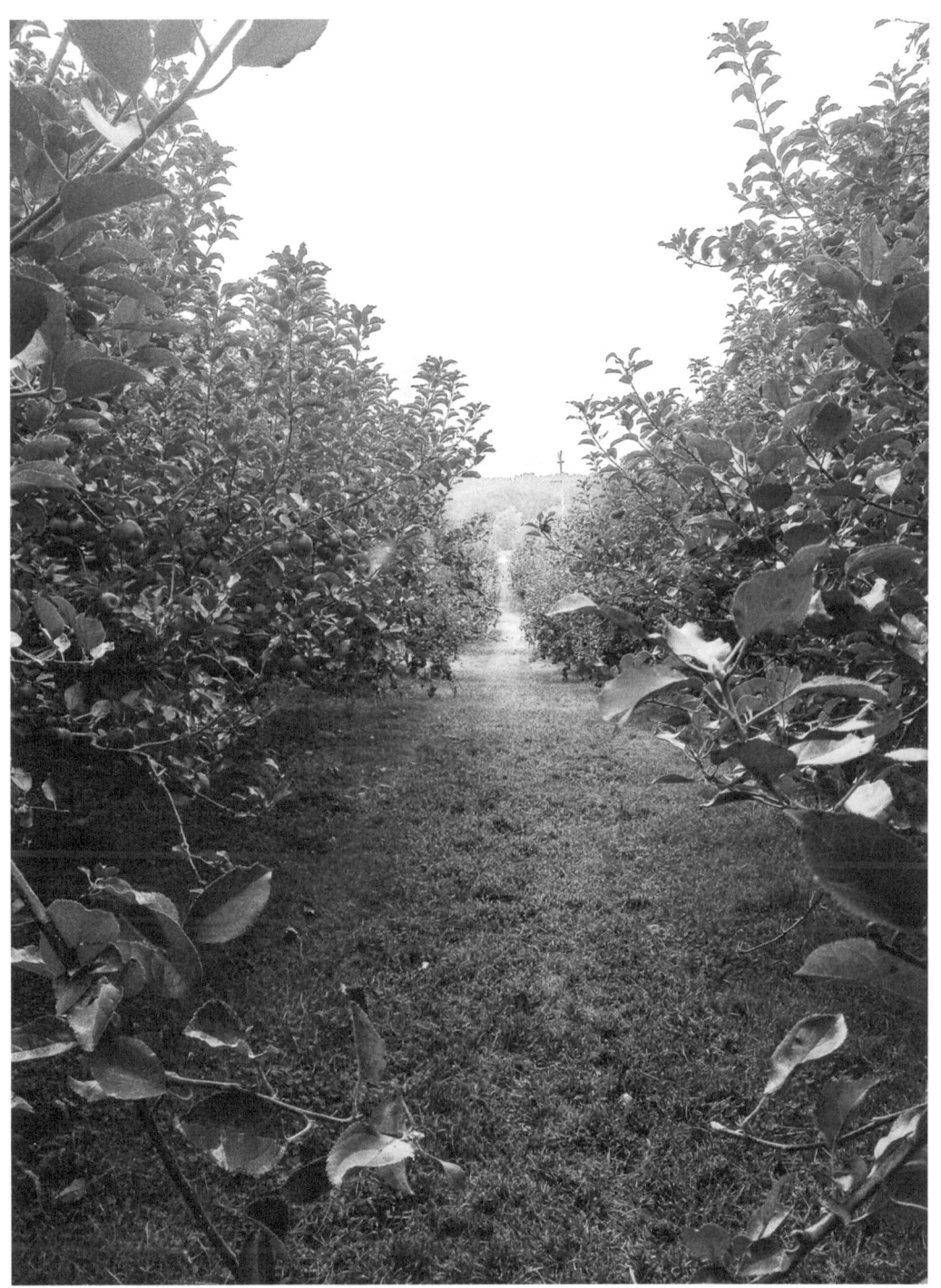

stephanie belluardo

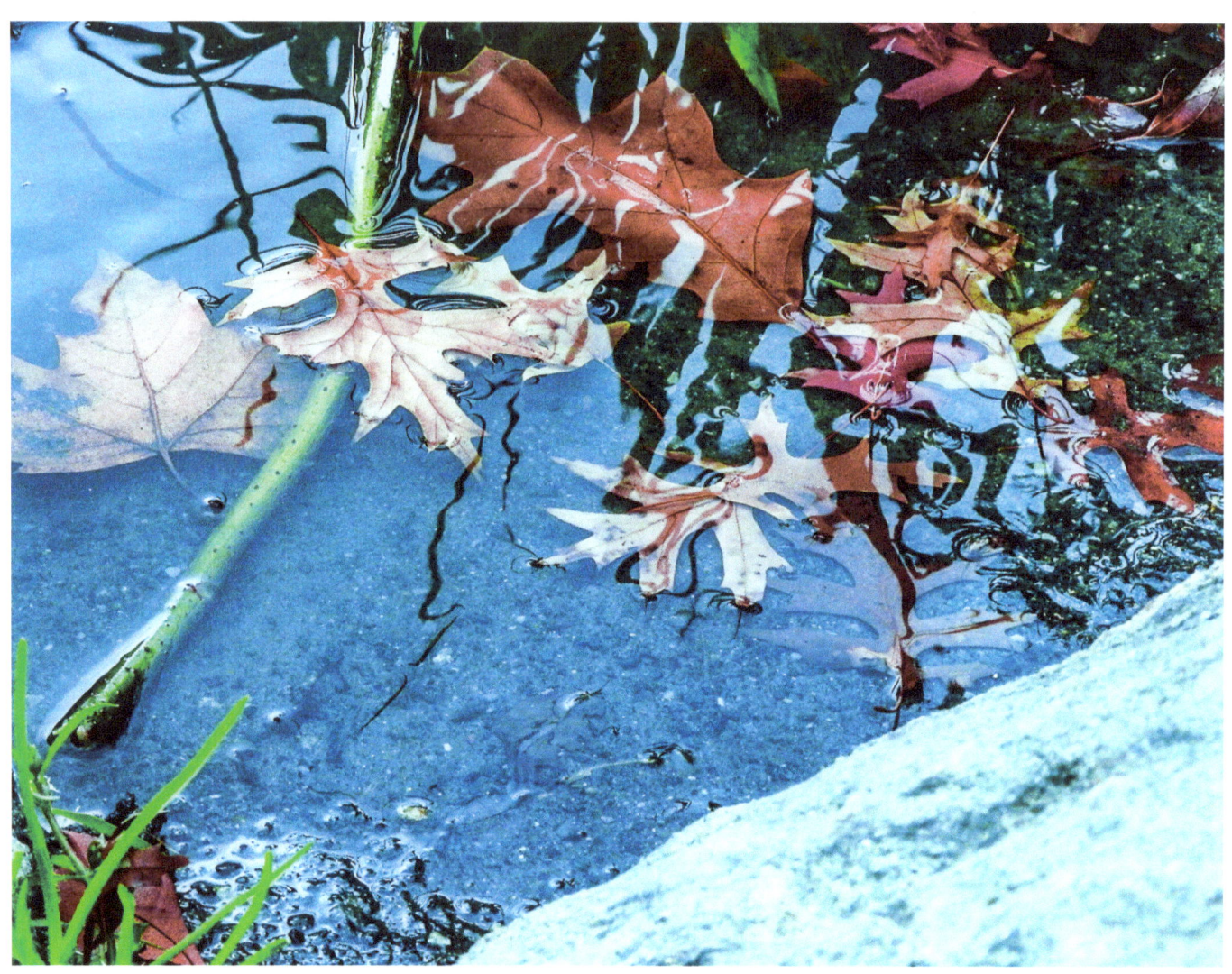

stephanie belluardo

the eyes that feel,

acosta, alicia
  luna.................................... 14
    digital, 5.627" x 7.5"
  candy creepolina......................... 15
    digital, 7.5" x 7.293"

belluardo, stephanie
  image #1................................. 26
    digital photograph, 10" x 7.69"
  image #2................................. 27
    digital photograph, 10" x 7.69"
  image #3................................. 28
    digital photograph, 7.58" x 10"
  image #4................................. 29
    digital photograph, 7.69" x 10"
  image #5................................. 30
    digital photograph, 10" x 7.58"

hoyle, jesse
  (un) ties #2.............................. 2
    photographic toner on beeswax and cedar,
    approximately 3.5" x 3.5" each
  (un) ties #1.............................. 3
    photographic toner on beeswax and cedar,
    approximately 3.5" x 3.5" each
  always (never) there..................... 4
    cyanotype, thread, paper, 5.5" x 11.5"
  artifact of place #9..................... 5
    silver gelatin print (pinhole photograph),
    8.5" 5.75"

juras, katherine
  thanks................................... 6
    digital, 6" x 6"
  love..................................... 7
    mixed media, 15" x 6"
  teapot................................... 8
    watercolor, 20" x 14"

stultz, bethany
  it's all clear........................... 10
    acrylic and watercolor, 9" x 12.125"
  pupils as deep as wells.................. 11
    acrylic and watercolor, 9" x 12.125"
  i'm a crazy acrobat...................... 12
    acrylic and watercolor, 9" x 12.125"
  mignonette............................... 13
    acrylic and watercolor, 7" x 10"

taber, rachel
  creek in the woods....................... 20
    charcoal on paper, 16" x 22"
  dandelion................................ 21
    charcoal on paper, 16" x 22"

teague, sarah
  isold.................................... 9
    acrylic and sand on wood, 7" x 9"
  girls without arms....................... 25
    altered dolls, 11.5" each

thomas, christopher
  giorno................................... 16
    ink on paper, 80" x 90"
  tomato cage icicles...................... 17
    pen and ink, 37" x 53"
  (dot) mathias............................ 18
    ink on paper, 80" x 52"
  (dot) mathias............................ 19
    detail

tisdell, suzanne
  venus.................................... 22
    oil on canvas, 12" x 9"
  danae.................................... 23
    charcoal, 22" x 30"
  dionysus................................. 24
    oil on canvas, 24" x 36"

the hands that see

to contact "the eyes that feel, the hands that
see" featured in the 2014 volume of the *starving
artist*, please write to:

the starving artist
little acorn associates, inc.
post office box 8787
greensboro, nc 27419-0787

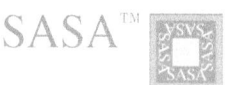

the starving artist
eyes that feel, hands that see
is a by-invitation publication

to be considered for inclusion,
please write to:

SASA™
Post Office Box 8787
Greensboro, North Carolina 27419-0787

www.ingramcontent.com/pod-product-compliance
Lightning Source LLC
Chambersburg PA
CBHW040451220526
45473CB00004B/1600